HIS

MASTERPIECE

Understanding Your True Worth as a Woman

By Ebony Ali

mechanical methods, without the prior written permission of the publisher, except in the case of brief quotations embodied in critical reviews and certain other non-commercial uses permitted by copyright law.

Published by

Editorial Services by Heritage Editing Services

www.heritageediting.co.uk

Disclaimer

Please note that in preparing this work, I have attempted to describe events, locations, and in many instances, I have had to create conversations from my memories of what happened at the time. To protect their identity, I have changed the names of many individuals and places. I may also have changed or fictionalised certain identifying characteristics and details, including physical appearances, occupations and places of residence.

Table of Contents

Introduction

In some tribal societies, before marriage, a man must pay something called the Bride Price (also known as a dowry) to the woman's family; usually a sum of money or goods that represent the woman's value.

I want to understand my worth, and I want you to understand yours.

God made us in his image. We were created to have dominion. We are called to reign as kings and queens with Christ. "Be fruitful, and multiply, and replenish the earth, and subdue it: and have dominion over the fish of the sea, and over the fowl of the air, and over every living thing that moveth upon the earth' (Genesis 1:28 KJV)." To live without fulfilling our God-ordained purpose would be a colossal tragedy.

In popular culture, diamonds are described as 'a girl's best friend' because they can make women feel financially secure and beautiful. Diamonds have largely come to symbolize love and commitment, so, when a man gives a woman a diamond ring, she feels valued.

Three components are needed to form diamonds: heat, pressure and time. Diamonds can take between 1-3.3 billion years to develop. Formed by heat and pressure, diamonds are then delivered to the earth's surface by deep-source volcanic eruptions or the movement of subduction zones that bring them up to the ocean floor. Diamonds can also be produced from the immense heat and pressure of asteroid strikes.

Diamonds require environments of at least 752 degrees Fahrenheit (400 degrees Celsius) and 434,113 pounds per square inch (30 kilobars). The most favourable diamond-forming conditions can be found about 100 miles (160 kilometres) underground.

God made us in his image. We were created to have dominion. We are called to rule and reign as kings and queens with Christ. To live without fulfilling our God-ordained purpose would be a colossal tragedy.

Not only are diamonds by far the most sought-after gemstones, coloured diamonds are the most expensive in the world. The rare and spectacularly brilliant blue diamond, worth 3.93 million dollars per carat, is the hardest substance found on earth.

His Masterpiece is written to help women see themselves the way God sees them. As stated in the book of Proverbs, the worth of a virtuous woman is very high because she is difficult to find. Just like a coloured diamond, she is a rare jewel! The Bible further states that the value of a good woman is even more than a coloured diamond.

1 Peter 1:18-19 (NIV) says,

> 'For you know that it was not with perishable things such as silver and gold that you were redeemed from the empty way of life handed down to you from your ancestors, but with the precious blood of Christ, a lamb without blemish or defect.'

This Scripture shows us that God has paid a bride price that cost him everything – his very life – for us!

We must constantly remind ourselves of this (His) truth whenever we doubt our worth and value. Seeking validation from any other source will only leave us disappointed. Material possessions do not satisfy, and our value in the eyes of others is subject to change.

While writing this book, I was tested on the very topic on which I hoped to share some truths. I've been as transparent about my experiences as possible in order to relate to my readers. If you do not understand your worth or need reminding, then I hope this book will be a blessing to you. You are worthy because God says you are and that, my darling, is something to rejoice about.

In my usual writing style, this book offers practical advice, poetry, spiritual guidance, as well as anecdotes from my personal experiences. I pray the book ministers to you, and that you allow it to take you on a journey of self-discovery and inner healing.

Sing, barren woman,

you who never bore a child;
burst into song, shout for joy,

you who were never in labor;
because more are the children of the desolate woman

than of her who has a husband,"
says the LORD.

Recommended read- Isaiah 54

Acknowledgements

I would like to thank my God and King Yahweh for helping me complete this book. The journey writing this was far from easy. There were many low points, more than I've cared to share. It took great courage – more than I knew I had in me –to complete this book. It was birthed through pain but inspired by love.

God has revealed my worth to me. It has gone from head- to heart-knowledge. He allowed me to see that my identity is in being his beloved bride, not the amount of money I make; my marital status or title as an author, or what others may say and think about me. It is not in my weaknesses, failures, or even my greatest successes.

Not only did he choose me, He still chooses me every day. I pray that, like a tree, I will continue to be deeply rooted in the knowledge of his steadfast love for me.

I also want to say thank you to a few friends who supported me during this journey.

Nellia, thank you for all your prayers, love, the many prophecies and wise counsel. It went a long way.

Thank you, Ren, for being there to pick up the pieces every time I fell apart. I can never forget how you spoke life and truth to me when I needed to hear it most.

Dedication

I would like to dedicate this book to my younger self: Dearest Ebony, I hope you will come to realise you were always enough. Even when you thought you were not, you were. You were never less than worthy.

I also want to dedicate this to my present self: It's been a long journey but look at you now, becoming who God made you to be. Well done, brave woman!

To my future self: I can't wait to meet you, Queen.

To my future biological and spiritual daughters and granddaughters: I want you to know that you are precious, valuable and loved by God and me. When it seems like the world is against you, please remember it 'hated him FIRST' and that 'if GOD is FOR you, WHO can be AGAINST you?' (Romans 8:31)

The answer is no one. You were born to thrive, flourish and shine.

I pray you do precisely that.

I love you!

Chapter 1: Kiss chase

'Dear children, keep yourselves from idols' (1 John 5:21 NIV).

An idol is not necessarily a statue that you bow down and worship, but anything that takes God's place in your life. Every heart has a throne. Whoever or whatever is sitting on the throne of your heart is what you value most.

We all have idols. Something or someone is fighting for our attention. 'Those who cling to worthless idols turn away from God's love for them' (Jonah 2:8 NIV).

Idols are worthless and, when we pursue them, they steal our worth (2 Kings 17:15 NLT). It takes spiritual enlightenment to recognise when we are chasing idols because it's normal in the world we live in, and it can be a huge surprise when we realise this.

The only cure for idol worship is **repentance**, translated from the Greek word *metanoia*. The literal meaning of *metanoia* is 'a change of mind'. 'Meta' means 'change'. 'Noia[1]' means 'mind'.

To be free from idol worship, we must change our minds about absolutely everything and teach ourselves to think as God thinks. We must begin to

---

[1]

http://www.Biblelineministries.org/articles/basearch.php?action=full&mainkey=REPENTANCE

unravel the web of lies in our minds about God, relationships, and ourselves. I'm still working on this.

Kiss chase

It's a game we played in primary school, where little boys and girls ran around the playground trying to kiss one another. As silly as it was, we all did it. I heard funny stories of children who targeted and seized the opportunity to smooch their crush. I was never kissed at that age. I was just happy to experience the adrenaline rush we felt as little boys and girls; black, white, Asian, and mixed-race, running around the playground excitedly, pigtails swinging, lots of giggling, an array of red and white uniforms as we shot by.

Martin Luther King Jr. would have been so proud.

Yes, we played kiss chase in primary school, but doesn't it seem like we never stopped playing this game? Those children simply grew into teenagers and matured into adults who are more skilled at it.

I cringe as I think back to all the times, I chased boys who sometimes did not want to be caught; all the times I've gone looking for love in the wrong places. The world tells me I just need 'the one' and, once I've found him, I will be complete. So, I'm disappointed when I meet the wrong one because, although it's a different guy it's the same story and I end up concluding, as I always do, no one is worthy to sit on the throne of my heart but God.

Where it all began

From as early as seven years old, I daydreamed about love and pictured my future self, married with children. Perhaps I watched too many Disney movies, but the idea of being in love exhilarated me.

Tremaine, my first crush, joined my primary school in Year Three. He was from Jamaica, chestnut in complexion, and wore his hair in twists. Good looking, popular and funny, the perfect candidate for a first crush.

We briefly played the boyfriend and girlfriend game when we were in Year Six, at ten years of age. After he had 'dated' a couple of my friends, it was my turn. We were good friends, so I was surprised when Tremaine invited me to our school's Valentine's Day disco. I felt special to have finally been selected to date one of the most popular boys in my year group. My mum agreed we could go together, and I was filled with nervous excitement as I waited for him and his mum to arrive at my house the night of the disco.

Tremaine flashed me a boyish grin as he made his way upstairs into our living room. My mum offered him a drink, and before he could respond, she was already in the kitchen.

Nervously, we stood there looking at each other as if we were thinking of something to say.

'Your mum has a lot of CD's.' he said, pointing towards my mum's impressive three-rack CD collection, all of which were taller than the both of us.

I smiled. 'I know.'

It was puppy love.

That night at the disco, a girl called Kamara sang *Dilemma* by Kelly Rowland and the rapper Nelly on the karaoke machine. Although Tremaine didn't know it, I decided that would be 'our song.' It's crazy how music can make you create stories in your head and bring out feelings you never knew you had.

My primary school was a 15-minute walk from my grandparents' house. Because Tremaine took a similar route home, we sometimes walked together with my younger sister. He would tell me about the video games he liked to play at home, this interested me because I also enjoyed playing video games.

'Do you want to have a look at them at my house one day after school?' He asked me.

'I'll have to ask my mum first.' was my response.

Mum agreed on the condition that my younger sister Hannah went with us. So, one evening after school, Tremaine's mum picked us up in her grey car and drove us to their house. Hannah and I spent the evening awkwardly hanging out in his room watching him play video games. On the way back home, his mum bought us all *KFC*, and he gave me a box of *After Eight* chocolates as a parting gift. That was the first time a boy had ever given me a gift.

Our childish romance was disrupted when my mother told my sister and me that we were moving to America to live with her older brother. I was heartbroken because it meant leaving all my friends and Tremaine behind. We said our goodbyes and I received a lovely leaving card from everybody at school. We were approaching the end of the academic year, about to take the SATs – our end of year exams. The SATs were used to evaluate a child's educational progress before secondary school. However, our sudden move meant that I couldn't take the exams. Mum didn't seem too concerned about this, perhaps because my teachers had always told her how capable I was.

However, things didn't go according to plan in America, and we returned to the UK after two and a half weeks, so it ended up being a short holiday instead. Although I enjoyed the trip, I was so relieved to be going back home.

On *May 16th*, the day we were heading home, I asked Mum if I could call Tremaine because it was his birthday. She gave me some change, and I called him from a payphone.

'Happy Birthday, Tremaine!' I said on his voicemail. 'I'm calling you from the airport. Guess what? I'm coming back to London!'

To my shock, when I returned, I discovered that Tremaine was 'in a relationship' with yet another girl in our class. I was surprised that he had moved on in such a short period and I guess you could say I felt less than unique. This was when I first began to understand what the word 'player' meant. I was too young to interpret my heartbreak, but I was unhappy during our end of year trip away. Noticing I had become withdrawn, my Year Six teacher asked me what was wrong.

'Nothing,' I responded.

She gave me a huge hug. It was good to know I was still loved, despite feeling like a disposable bin bag. Easily replaceable.

Tremaine taught me that boys could be such fickle beings.

––––––––

I'm not sure exactly when my obsession with the RNB rapper, Bow Wow, began, but I was infatuated with him in secondary school. It had to be the longest game of *kiss chase* I ever played. Without trying to sound like a stalker, admiring someone from afar can be comforting. Perhaps it's because they can never reject us.

I labelled myself as Mrs Shad Gregory Moss, aka, 'Bow Wow's future wifey', and imagined that every song he released was specially written for me. One Valentine's Day, I wrote a twelve-page letter declaring my undying love for him and sent it to his record label. I used hot pink paper and wrote it in my neatest handwriting, hoping he would read it and know that somebody loved him. I'd even calculated the age gap between us (he was six years older) and rationalised when I would be old enough to date him. On his birthday (March 9th), I would announce at school: 'Everyone, today is Bow Wow's birthday!' while mindlessly scrolling through pictures of him on the internet in my IT class.

During school breaks, there were heated debates between my friend, Shanelle and I about who was his true love.

'Shanelle, we all know that **I** am Bow wow's future wifey!' I said half-jokingly.

'No, what do you mean? **I am** Bow wow's future wifey!' She would yell back defiantly.

'We'll see.' I made sure I had the last word.

I was so sure I was real 'wifey material'; convinced that, if I hoped enough, he would be mine one day. I even once posted on his fan page stating that, unlike the other girls who admired him, I just wanted him to be happy. Even if that meant he was in a relationship with Ciara (a famous musician he was dating at the time) and not me.

It was a real, albeit, one-sided relationship. There were laminated and print-out posters of him around my room, and I was up to date with all his new music, meditating on it day and night. I guess you could say he was my god.

I'm sure most teenage girls (and grown women, if we're honest), can relate to this kind of obsessive behaviour since we now stalk men on social media.

— — — — — — —

When I moved schools in 2009, I had a massive crush on a boy called Isaiah in my year group. I'm not sure what attracted me to him. He was scrawny, so it must have been his beautiful face, chocolate skin and long cornrows which were styled all back. He reminded me of Lloyd, the RNB singer.

He hung around with a guy called Moe. Moe was gigantic – he was probably the same size as I imagined Lennie, the character described as 'a huge man who walked heavily', in the book *Of Mice and Men* to be. Isaiah looked like an ant next to Moe.

Moe found out I liked Isaiah and tried to make him talk to me. Isaiah looked so bashful as he tried to squirm his way from Moe's grasp.

'I don't want to talk to her.' He said, looking directly at me. 'She's butters.' Butters was a slang term for ugly.

I don't think what Isaiah thought of me made a difference to me at the time; I just knew I liked him.

Why chase after a boy who couldn't even see my beauty?

Could it be because *I* couldn't see it, either? What I didn't understand back then was how much I needed a guy to validate me. I know I'm not the only female to have experienced this.

Fast forward to my first year at university, when I developed a huge crush on Callum in the year above me. He was fair in complexion with a chiselled face and handsome features. He was also friendly, ambitious and talented. Most girls agreed that he was good-looking.

When a friend introduced us, Callum said he remembered my name from registration, during fresher's week. I had signed up for the African Caribbean Society, for which he happened to be a key representative.

'Ebony Ali... yeah, I remember your name. It sounds like someone famous.'

You can imagine how pleased I was to hear that!

I once went to an event where he was the ticket administrator. I remember gazing into his eyes as he handed me my wristband. Seconds later, I was halfway up the stairs, excitedly shrieking to my friends, 'Did you see Callum...? Did you see Callum?' I pretended I was going to faint.

If I could have a conversation with my younger self, I would be upfront and tell her: 'All of this because of a guy, Ebony? Pull yourself together, Girl!'

Having a crush makes life interesting. It's only dangerous when your crush starts to crush you because he has become an idol. One evening, I was with some Christian friends at university, and we started discussing silly things we did for guys we liked in the past. One of the girls told a story about a guy in college.

'I did his coursework.' she exclaimed.

I looked at her in disbelief, but I was no different. Women do some foolish things when we like someone.

Obsession—that's what we were taught that love is, isn't it? Chemical reactions in your brain, making you feel higher than any drug could. Love must be equal to obsession, right?

Wrong.

Often, we're just using the other person to fill the void inside.

A popular phrase we use to describe someone desperate for love today is 'thirsty'. It reminds me of the Samaritan woman in the Bible who met Jesus by a well. Jesus says something so profound to her.

'Jesus answered her. "If you knew the gift of God and who it is that asks you for a drink, you would have asked him, and he would have given you living water"' (John 4:10 NIV).

He recognised that this 'thirsty' woman had a profound spiritual thirst that only He could satisfy.

'Jesus answered, "Everyone who drinks this water will be thirsty again, but whoever drinks the water I give them will never thirst. Indeed, the water I give them will become in them a spring of water welling up to eternal life"' (John 4:13-14 NIV).

The goal is to be filled with so much of God that we no longer use natural means to quench our spiritual appetite. 'Blessed are those who hunger and thirst for righteousness, for they will be filled' (Matthew 5:6 NIV).

It reminds me of the testimony a young woman shared on an Instagram video. She was a Christian but had slept with guys because she wanted them to like her. I could see myself in this woman, as I too have entertained such thoughts to keep men around.

One thing she said that stood out to me was, 'I was paying for something that had already been freely given to me.'

Back to the Samaritan woman:

'He told her, "Go, call your husband and come back." "I have no husband," she replied. Jesus said to her, "You are right when you say you have no husband. The fact is, you have had five husbands, and the man you now have is not your husband. What you have just said is quite true.' John 4:16-18 NIV)

The Samaritan woman had been married many times, and now she was in a 'situationship' because she was thirsty for love. Now here was Jesus offering her the solution to her problems, free of charge.

Would she accept his request? Will you?

(You can find out what happens to this Samaritan Woman in the rest of the book of John 4:19-30).

In 1 Corinthians 13:4-8, the Bible says,

'Love is patient,
Love is kind.

It does not envy [*But I thought jealousy was a sign of love?*]

It does not boast. [*But I thought if I loved someone, I needed to boast about myself to impress them?*]

It is not proud. [*How can I forgive him so easily?*]

It does not dishonour others. [*Men are trash*]

It is not self-seeking. [*What do I get from loving you?*]

It is not easily angered. [*But why hasn't he texted me back?*]

It keeps no record of wrongs. [*If this is true, why am I holding others' shortcomings against them? Why am I holding my shortcomings against myself?*]

Love does not delight in evil but rejoices with the truth. It always protects. Always trusts, always hopes, always perseveres. LOVE NEVER FAILS.'

The opposite of this is lust. Lust is all about immediate gratification, appealing to a person's ego and selfish nature with a strong emphasis on physical attraction but no real depth. Love develops with time and knowledge. It is when you genuinely see value in another human being and want to give more than you receive.

Oh boy, am I in trouble. I am yet to grasp what love is.

Why do us women always seem to easily fall for men who **want** but do not *deserve* us? There are many reasons why I believe this happens, all of which I will explore in this book.

Chapter 2: Broken but not shattered

Broken, that's the only way to describe the way I felt towards the end of December 2019. It had been a great year of acceleration and favour, but the choices I made towards the end of the year left me feeling broken and alone.

The days leading up to Christmas were filled, not with joy and laughter, but with depression and despair. I lay in bed, distraught and filled with regret at every decision that had brought me to this point. Once again, I had allowed myself to get emotionally attached to the wrong man.

Trying to cling to my idol, a couple of days after Christmas, I decided to reach out to David again. I badgered him with texts and phone calls asking him to meet up. I knew better but didn't want to face the reality of my brokenness.

What led me here?

Have you ever felt so broken that you wonder if you will ever be whole? Will you ever feel like yourself again?

I felt worthless. Worthless because that's how they always leave me feeling in the end. These idols. But that doesn't stop me from craving their attention. Even though I had my suspicions that David's intentions were not pure from the beginning, I wanted it to be love.

Why?

Love is the reason we live. Isn't Love what we all want and need? And oh, how desperately we cling to the shadows that masquerade as glimmers of light and hope.

You know how it starts: boy meets girl, girl plays hard to get but secretly enjoys the attention. Boy does all he can to impress her.

I met David at a church conference abroad. I was new to the church, but he had been in it for a while.

Our conversation was friendly and brief. When we got back to the UK, he made several attempts to talk to me through social media or in person at our church gatherings. To begin with, I found his advances hilarious.

He sent friendly messages on Instagram asking why I didn't tell him I had a book out and how 'that was big'. Trying to keep the conversation God-centred, I said 'God was big'. He agreed.

Then I received a text message late one night asking me if I was Jacob. When I replied that I was not, he said he had texted a wrong number he got off Instagram and asked me why my number was up there. I didn't respond to the message and simply removed my phone number from Instagram. I had recently turned my page into a business account, and I must have made my number public by mistake.

Looking back, David's story didn't make sense. Jacob was one of his close friends, so why would he text *me*? Especially if he found the number on my Instagram page.

He started messaging me more often. Sometimes, it was about his conversations with other church members discussing how amazing I was. Mostly, he asked if I got home safely after church. I can't deny that it made me feel good, but I didn't think it would lead anywhere. I sometimes sent him a voice note (it was easier than responding to texts), and he would make a big deal about how nice my voice sounded and ask if I was trying to hypnotise him.

I laughed, confused.

One day after church, we were all hanging out as a group, and David accidentally poured water on my jeans.

'I'm so sorry, let me get you a tissue.'

'It's fine. It's only water. It will dry.' I replied. I let him get the tissue anyway.

'Wow, I can't believe you're not mad. My ex would have been so mad.' He looked mesmerized.

I should have seen the red flag right there. *Why was he comparing me to his ex?*

When I got home that evening, he messaged, as usual, to check if I got back safely.

I did, thank you.

Sorry again, about the water.

It's fine. Honestly, it was an accident. Naively, I sent him a hug emoji to reassure him.

Do you want to come and make that real?

I was stunned by his response. *What was going on?*

The first evening he called me after church, I realised just how determined this guy was.

'Ebony, I'm not looking to be in a relationship right now. Maybe way in the future. If I'm going to be with someone, I need to take the time to get to know them. I want to be friends with the person first. So, I want to get to know you as a friend.'

I was intrigued. 'You want to be my friend, yeah? Interesting.' I said.

'How is that interesting?'

'It just is. I don't think I can be your friend.'

'Why not?'

'I don't have time for this right now.'

'Neither do I.'

'I want to focus on myself and my relationship with God.' I continued. It sounded like the right thing to say, and at the time, I thought I meant those words.

'I get it. We're both busy people.' He replied. 'As I said, I just want to be friends.'

'Okay.'

'Tell me, when were you last in a relationship?'

I didn't like where this was going.

'I'm not trying to have pillow talk with you.' I said.

'What? That's not what I'm trying to do here. I'm not even in my bed.'

That evening we ended up talking for three hours.

It was as though a magnetic force was drawing me to him. I tried to put boundaries between us because there were lines, I didn't want to cross but, as the weeks went by, the more we spoke over the phone, the harder it got. David told me he worked in sales, he was charming and had a way with words, so I was sure he would be good at his job. He knew how to get what he wanted, and I could tell that he wanted me.

One night, he told me he had a vision of us eating in *Vapianos*, one of my favourite restaurants.

'You were even wearing your black hat.' He said.

'It's never going to happen,' I told him. 'Keep dreaming.'

'I will keep dreaming... because dreams can become a reality.' He replied.

'Sit next to me at the meeting tomorrow.' He told me.

'Okay.'

We hung up.

––––––––

The next day, in the morning, I went to a Christian business seminar with Alfred, one of my friends from church. David and I kept messaging each other throughout the day. I liked how consistent he was.

When you sit next to me tonight, it's going to be a wrap.

Our church was holding an annual conference and we were having a meeting that night in order to prepare.

I laughed out loud.

What are you going to do? There are other people there.

I was still finding it all funny at this point.

I don't care about them.

When I arrived at church, I sat next to him as instructed.

He handed me an open packet of Skittles. 'I got these for you.'

'Thank you.' I knew he hadn't, but free food is free food, right?

The meeting began, but I was distracted by the texts he kept sending me, although we were next to each other. I was wearing my infamous black hat. I had also taken the time to look extra lovely and had worn red lipstick and straightened my hair.

You could say I was dancing with the devil at this point.

Your hair looks nice.

Thanks.

He turned to me. "I bet you were waiting for me to say that."

I rolled my eyes.

He continued to text me.

Let me wine and dine you.

No.

That's not what you want, is it?

What do you want from me?

A lot... but we'll get to that later.

What makes you think I should give you a lot?

I'm not saying you should. I'm just telling you what I want.

KMT[2]

I won't kiss your teeth unless you want me to.

No, you need to stop.

It was getting harder to resist his advances.

— — — — — — — —

The next day I sent him a voice note.

'I can't keep on putting out these fires you're trying to light. We need to keep things pure.'

'What did I do now?' he responded. I could tell he was enjoying this. 'Okay, maybe I was a little cheeky. But I don't think I did anything wrong.'

My head was spinning; I was losing control bit by bit.

I knew I needed a man who was more devoted to God than David appeared to be, but what he had to offer seemed worth the risk. He filled my mind with promises of dates and special treatment and told me stories of all the wonderful things he did for his ex-

---

[2] KMT is a slang term meaning "Kiss My Teeth" used to express genuine or fake annoyance, disgust or disdain.

girlfriend. The thing is, I suspected he would deliver on his word but wasn't sure if I wanted to date him and didn't want to take advantage.

I always said no, but I also started to develop feelings for him, or at least what he had to offer. He wasn't the usual type of guy I would go for, but I knew I wasn't his type, either. He told me that he usually went for 'rave girls' – whatever that meant. But, since his breakup, he was looking more at the woman's characteristics, and he knew what he wanted now.

'My ex was gorgeous, but her character wasn't right.' He told me. 'It was a toxic relationship. I went through 3 years of hell so, as soon as I see any red flags, I'm out of here. I'm looking for a woman who has the fruits of the Spirit.'

'What are they?' I asked.

'You know, like you do...' He rattled off the list. 'Love, patience, kindness…'

I told you he had a way with words.

It was all flattering but felt too much, too soon, and I tried to cut him off several times. I asked him to block me. I even got my mentor to have a word with him.

He called me immediately after he got off the phone to her. 'I've never heard her so angry, so I'm going to leave you alone. I don't want to cause any trouble.'

'It's for the best.' I said. 'Besides, we'll still see each other at church.'

'Ok.' He said and hung up. Two minutes later, he called back. 'There's one last thing I want to say; I had nothing but good intentions.' He sounded sad and hung up again.

He blocked me on WhatsApp, so I thought it was over. Until he messaged me on Instagram a few days later with a church-related question.

I responded courteously, but I was upset, so I sent him another message.

You might as well block me on here.

He sent me a voice note.

'Ebony, please don't make this harder than it needs to be.' He said. 'It was upsetting to do that, but I had no choice.'

I was triggered.

Do you think it's just hard for you, it's hard on me too.

I pressed send and blocked him. I was not practising any self-control at this point.

Although hadn't been speaking very long, a part of me didn't want to let go because of the potential of what this could become.

That night, I cried. Again, I thought it was over.

Until he rang me the next day.

I had just left my full-time job and was considering my next move. In the interim, I decided to volunteer at a mental health women's group in Sutton.

I saw I had missed a call from an unknown number, so I called back.

'Hello, who is this?'

'Who do you think it is?'

'David, how are you? I didn't recognise your number.'

'This is my other phone.' He said. 'Did you block me on Instagram?'

'Yeah, I did.'

He laughed.

'You know, I'm in Sutton.' I said, 'I'm volunteering at this mental health charity.'

'Whereabouts?'

'Belmont.' I responded.

'That's about 10 minutes away from where I live.' He said. 'Do you want to see me afterwards?'

'Okay, I'll message you when I'm done.'

There it was again, that nervous excitement, I could hardly wait for my shift to end.

I need to go to the post office.

I'll take you. Do you want me to cook for you?

No, I'm not hungry.

He sent me directions and asked me to message him when I was three stops away from the station near his house.

It was drizzling when I got to the station, so I sent him a message.

Don't leave me waiting in the rain.

It took him seven minutes to arrive.

'I had to run here.' He said. 'My car's currently in the garage. If I had known you were coming, I would have driven my dad's car to pick you up.'

'Aww, thanks.' I said. 'I need to print this return label out so I can send these back.' I showed him the bag of clothes I had bought from a website online.

'You can do that at my house.'

So, I went to his house. He offered me biscuits and lunch, but I wasn't that hungry. I accepted the hot chocolate he made instead.

'I missed talking to you.' I told him.

'Maybe one of your pastor friends will take you out.' He replied.

He'd previously asked me what I wanted in a man. I said I wanted a prayerful man and that I wanted to marry a pastor.

'Do you know that half of these Pastors cheat on their wives?' He had responded. 'It's disgusting, and I'm sick of it. Ebony, you don't want to marry a Pastor. You want someone fun.'

'That's just what men say when they don't want to live up to your standards.' I said.

'Okay, how about someone who isn't a Pastor but who wants to support homeless people.' He reasoned.

He got me there.

'I guess ministry can be done in different ways.'

— — — — — — — —

I noticed lots of messages about faith and God in his living room. His parents were devout believers, so that didn't surprise me.

'Have you seen our collection of books over here?' He asked, picking one up to show me the front cover. It was about the end times. 'You can borrow one if you like.'

I knew he was trying to impress me. 'Do you even read them, or are they your parents'?' I asked.

He smiled.

I printed out the label. Then as we stood at the bottom of the staircase, ready to head out, I had a sudden flashback. Something about this situation felt strangely familiar. It reminded me of being at a guy's house when I was supposed to be in school. The guy with whom I shared my first kiss had somehow convinced me to skip school and visit him. He also persuaded me to do things I found uncomfortable. Being with David also reminded me of a male friend I had in school, that I felt sorry for. He had told me he had a medical condition and wasn't going to live very long, so I came to the rescue and visited his house any time he was bored. It was a strange friendship.

I had already told David he made me feel uncomfortable.

'I don't like that word.' He replied. 'Do you mean that I make you feel shy? I think you are very comfortable around me.'

He was partially right, but it was a false sense of comfort. I was equally as scared. Isn't that normal when you like someone?

What a mess.

It was still raining slightly when we left.

'Do you want to wear one of my coats?' He asked.

'No, I'm good.'

As we walked to the post office, David started telling me more about himself – what kind of snacks and drinks he liked. He also mentioned he was having some medical problems with his heart and that he had nearly fainted the other day.

When we arrived, the post office queue was quite long.

'I need to leave soon because I'm tutoring my cousin today.' I said.

'You're tutoring now? What do you tutor in?' he asked.

'Maths and English.'

'You must be smart to tutor those subjects.'

'Not that smart.' I replied.

'What did you get for your GCSEs?'

'I did alright. I got mostly B's.' I said.

'I didn't do well in school.' He murmured. 'That's why I'm so grateful I got the job I did.'

'Yes. Alfred says the same thing.' Alfred and David worked for the same company.

'You're always talking about Alfred.' He grumbled. 'What do you like about him?'

I could tell he was jealous, but it wasn't threatening. 'He was one of the first people to make me feel welcome when I joined the church.' I said. 'I like talking to him. He's intelligent and, besides, we're from the same country so we can banter.'

David smiled and stuck his tongue out the side of his mouth. 'Do you think I'm intelligent?'

'Why's your tongue out?' I responded. 'Of course, you are. You just want attention.'

He kept smiling.

'I think I'm going to post this another day,' I finally said. 'I need to get home so I can start my tutoring.'

We left the post office and headed towards the station. I resisted the urge to link arms with David.

'What happens now?' I asked as we waited for the train to arrive.

'The ball is in your court Ebony, look at how quickly I came to meet you today.' He said, looking intently into my eyes. 'We can either be friends, and I'll be cool with you, say 'Hi' at church; or you can be part of my life, and I'll treat you good.'

I panicked and immediately looked away. I couldn't think straight. I didn't want him giving me the cold-shoulder like before. But the way he stared at me made me scared and excited at the same time. *How was that even possible?*

'I'll have to pray about it.' I eventually replied.

'Pray about it, meditate on it. Do what you need to.' He said, leaning in to hug me goodbye.

I believe he meant it when he said he would treat me good. We had spent the afternoon together, and he was a 'perfect gentlemen.' I knew then that I wanted to be with him, but God had previously warned me not to engage with him on that level. What was I going to do now that I had caught feelings?

Our phone conversations continued, and I didn't have time to pray about it again. The closer we got, the further I drifted from God's presence. Instead of praying in the early hours of the morning, I would rather talk to David.

'Ebony, you're beginning to be like a drug.' He said.

'Don't say that!' I liked the fact that he felt good when he spoke to me, but the word drug didn't sound healthy.

The late-night phone calls were getting more and more intense.

'Do you like me... or are you just bored?' David asked.

'Yeah, I do.'

'What do you like about me?'

'I like that you're kind and smart and funny.'

That's how I felt. But did I like David or the attention he gave me? I hardly knew the guy. I could tell he just wanted to go with the flow, but I needed to make sense of the situation. It felt like we would eventually end up being 'friends with benefits' and that was not what I wanted. But I didn't want to look like I was overthinking things.

'What are we doing?' I asked him.

'We are just two people who like each other.' He shot back.

This made sense logically.

'You can speak to other guys if you want to,' he continued. 'I just want to continue getting to know you.'

But I had already fully invested my emotions. I started to ask people around me for advice. As time went on, I started to feel trapped, so I went to stay with Julie for a couple of nights to clear my head. Julie was an older female I met at my friend Noel's Bible study. She was white, a brunette with curly hair. We had connected because she had a heart for feeding homeless people, for whom she cooked and served every Friday night. I had nicknamed her 'Mama Jules'.

'He sounds like a narcissist.' Julie said after I explained what was going on. 'Be careful.'

'What makes you say that?' I was curious to find out.

'I've experienced these types of men so many times. Read up on it.' She pointed at my hair which was in a state. 'Look at how much this is consuming you. You're losing yourself, and if you don't stop it now, he'll leave you in a much worse state, you'll be left on the floor.'

I laughed. It sounded dramatic. 'I've tried to insist we shouldn't talk so late, but David makes the excuse that he's up working those hours.'

'You know that's booty call time.' She replied. 'The thing is, my dear, you want to be loved, but that's not what he wants.'

That triggered a nerve, and a tear ran down my cheek. She was right. I did want love. He had told me from the beginning he wasn't looking to be in a relationship, but he did want to get to know me better as a 'friend.'

He messaged me again late that night, but I chose not to respond.

When he called the following Friday night, I picked it up.

We exchanged pleasantries.

'I thought I'd give you a call to see how you're doing.' He said. 'Seeing as you don't care if I'm alive.'

'I've been staying at my friend's house. You know we're not in a relationship,' I said firmly. 'I don't have to answer the phone every time you call.'

'Right.' He said petulantly.

'I'm just getting ready to go out.'

'Are you going to a party?'

'Have you forgotten who you're talking to?' I snapped.

'I have, actually.' He said. 'I'll leave you to get ready. Call me when you're free to talk.'

As soon as we hung up, all my insecurities started to flare up. It felt like I was going to have to become somebody I was not. David knew I was a dedicated Christian, so why would he suddenly think I was going to a party on a Friday night? Maybe that's what his ex-girlfriend did?

I texted him.

I'm going to a worship night; do you want to come?

He took a while to respond.

Why didn't you tell me earlier, dear?

I was trying to see how he would respond. I wanted him in my life, but I couldn't see how he fit into God's plan for me. We had spoken about God, but I wouldn't say he was the centre of our conversations.

New Year's Eve, which I usually spent in church, was approaching. He had mentioned that the previous year he went to see the fireworks with his ex. What if he suggested we do the same? Everything was happening so quickly, and we hadn't even been on a date.

That night, at the worship event, God told me through a minister that he wanted to use my writing to heal myself and help others. I cried a lot. I couldn't see how God still wanted to use me considering my current messy situation.

'What's stopping you from writing?' The minister asked me.

'I feel so ashamed.' I choked.

He looked at me, his eyes shining with compassion. 'Nothing you do can make me reject you.'

I could tell God was speaking through him. I thought back to earlier that year at another church event when a minister had told me he saw me being an example for women.

I spoke to David on the phone that evening.

'How was the event?' He asked.

'It was amazing! I received a prophecy that I am going to be an influential writer.'

'I'm happy for you.'

We carried on talking for another week. I still had my doubts about whether things could work but wanted to give David the benefit of the doubt.

—————————

The following Friday night, we talked on the phone as usual. I made sure we didn't talk for too long because he was supposed to wake up early to do something for church on Saturday morning. The plan was to meet in the afternoon. I was tutoring a student near where David lived in the morning, then going to my friend Esther's book launch and workshop, also in the area.

One of Esther's client's books was titled *Lord, is This Relationship for Me?* I knew I needed to purchase it.

David messaged me at the launch.

I asked if he did what he had to do at church that morning.

He told me he didn't because he woke up late after talking to someone special (me) till late. **[Idols]**.

That was the final straw. I didn't want to be a distraction for him and vice versa. I messaged him.

No one is more important than God.

That's true. I was upset that I couldn't go.

I don't think this is going to work.

Wow…

I need someone who loves God more than they like me.

What makes you say that? Give me examples.

Through your actions. I don't want to fight.

He messaged me again, but I didn't respond.

After the event, I poured my heart out to a lady called Pamela, one of the pastors at my church.

'I've been so angry with God.' I told her, tears rolling down my cheeks. I didn't realise how I had felt until the words came out of my mouth.

We spoke for a while in front of the hotel, and she encouraged me. I decided to get my nails painted at the nail shop and to attend a worship night happening in that area later. The worship night was powerful.

When I checked my phone, I had a missed call from David. He was expecting me to respond to his message. I didn't want the distraction. When the evening was over, I tried to call him. It was pouring with rain, and although it was selfish of me, I wanted to see if he would pick me up.

He didn't answer my call. Instead, he texted.

You called?

I waited till I got home till I replied.

I know you're upset, and you think I'm avoiding you, but that's not the case. I did want to explain what I meant.

You were obviously avoiding me. I'm human, not an emotionless robot. I think you're playing some kind of game and I'm not here for it.

If that's how you feel, you might as well block me. I hate hurting people.

I cried myself to sleep. I was expecting him to be done with the situation. I didn't want to break his heart. I guess, I had started to believe he had developed genuine feelings for me.

My phone vibrated at around four in the morning with a message:

You asleep?

I was barely awake, so I waited till I was up properly to respond.

Yes, I was, but now I need to get ready, I'm visiting my friend's church today.

Have a blessed day day.

I took my time to draft a clear message.

Look, what I was trying to say is that you say you want to get to know me but who are you accountable to? The foundation of a healthy relationship is not friendship but Christ. If you don't believe me, ask your parents or your leaders at church. I watched this video the other day. I'm not saying this is us, but this will better explain what I mean.

I sent him the link to a video of an American couple I found on YouTube. Their story was inspiring because they were initially in a relationship but separated because the girl decided to take God seriously, and the guy didn't. God eventually brought them back together.

I made my way to the church. Just as I was about to step into the church building, I received another message from David.

I will watch the video. We will talk later.

That Sunday, I broke down in tears at the altar. I knew God was telling me it was time to fully let go after I had ignored him so many times. I couldn't understand how I ended up in this situation in the first place. I was so emotionally attached.

The truth is, I may have felt like I was 'falling in love' with this man, but I didn't trust him enough to lead me.

I messaged him when I got home.

Let me know when it's a good time to talk.

He responded almost straight away. *Now is good.*

So, I called him.

'I don't think this is going to work.' I said.

'I feel like you've taken me on a rollercoaster ride, Ebony. Every time I think we're getting somewhere; you end up saying something like this.'

'I guess the ride has to come to an end eventually.' I told him. 'I told you I want to marry a pastor. I also think you need to work on your relationship with God.'

'How can you say I don't have a relationship with God?' He sounded shocked.

'If it offends you, maybe look at that. I can't speak to you now. Maybe in a month.'

'A month?'

'Yeah, and I'm going to block you.'

'Just like that?'

'I don't have a choice.' I said.

'Okay, I understand.' He said quietly. 'I guess you're just looking out for both parties. You already know what my conclusion is, but I have to respect your decision.'

'Okay, thank you. Bye.'

Looking back on that conversation, I was harsh, but I thought I was doing what was best for both of us.

Besides, it felt like he had somehow manipulated me. I had been so sure about what I wanted in a partner, but he said things that twisted my mind. I experienced a series of disappointments earlier that year with potential love interests, but this had to be the worst.

— — — — — — — —

Now that David was gone, my fears were speaking to me loud and clear. This question kept ringing in my head like an alarm clock that wouldn't switch off:

Who's going to love me now that you're gone?

I couldn't bring myself to look for the answer. Instead, I buried myself in my favourite TV shows and listened to songs that mirrored my pain and resentment.

Never again would I open up to a guy.

What I should have told myself was: *Never again would I listen to sweet words and ignore actions.*

Being busy just wasn't enough anymore. I had to face whatever was going on inside me. It felt like I was plummeting from Cloud Nine to my death on the ground.

It gets hard to breathe when your head is underwater. You start to lose hope. You begin to believe nobody will save you because you're not worth saving. I needed a lifeline. I was hoping that any minute now, someone would come along with a lifeboat and bring me back to shore.

Just when I started to lose consciousness, you spoke a word, breathed your life into me and brought me back to life again.

You shared your dreams with me - visions of our future together.

I started to see a light; initially a small spark, like a flicker of hope. As you kept speaking the light grew so bright, I was forced to open my eyes.

Eyes wide open, I looked into my hero's eyes and, to my surprise, they burned like shots of fiery flames of love.

The light was almost blinding.

As you continued to speak, the words coming from your mouth entered me.

You were giving me yourself.

Here's what I've learnt: Sometimes you don't get what you want because you deserve better.

Just because someone desires you does not mean they deserve you. To be the object of another's desire is a great thing. The attention can be intoxicating but, like too much wine, after a while, receiving attention from the wrong person does more damage than good.

Choose yourself again and again, instead of waiting for someone to choose you. Self-love goes hand in hand with self-respect. If you do not value yourself, you will settle for less than you deserve.

The brave thing doesn't always look brave at the time. Sometimes the most courageous thing you can do is to walk away.

Who's going to love me now that you're gone?

This is the most difficult question you have to answer once you've broken up with an idol. You must find the answer.

Chapter 3: Wholeness

When Lust looks like Love

I can't say that it will never happen again. I can only pray it won't, by the grace of God.

That the metamorphosis will be completed in me... so that, next time, I would be so full of love I won't settle for lust disguised as love.

It's like choosing a cheap handbag instead of an original. They look the same at first, but with time, you start to notice the fading quality: the letters drop off, the strap breaks, and you're left with the remains of something you once looked at with admiration.

Lust looks like love when you don't know what love truly is and lies sound like the truth when you don't know what the truth sounds like.

I'm speaking not just for myself but for every woman, who is also a girl. Every girl caught up in the arms of a guy who promises her the world on one condition: that she gives him parts of herself that she can never get back.

Parts of herself she wanted to give to someone special but gave it instead to someone who told her she was special. So, she convinced herself that risking it all was worth it. After all, he promised her the world.

What he didn't promise her was himself. He didn't offer his heart, loyalty and commitment. She temporarily had his attention, in exchange for pleasure, but not for a lifetime which, deep inside, is what she wanted.

She wanted the love that came with commitment and gave more than it took. Steadfast and consistent love that built up and didn't tear down. Not this emotional rollercoaster ride that, like a drug, made her feel so high but then so low.

She dreamed of a pure and whole love.

Of a man who chose her and wasn't looking for her to fill a void in himself.

Agape[3].

This love had to stand the test of time and let patience complete its work. He had to, like she was, be willing to risk it all.

It killed parts of her to realise this man couldn't give her what she wanted. Would she ever recover from the disappointment and dissatisfaction that came from realising he wasn't in it for love?

There was nothing she could do to change that. Her only choice was to heal. She didn't know what it would look or feel like, but she would eventually heal. She had been here before.

No matter what he took from her, there was nothing that couldn't be restored as long as she determined to rise again.

(Feb 2020)

---

[3] **Agape** is a biblical term for the highest of unconditional love – especially from God to man.

The evolution of me

The path to the whole self is never easy.

It requires a lot of death.

The death of specific behavioural patterns. i.e. putting up with all forms of abuse because 'I'm used to it.'

The death of making excuses for others.

The death of people-pleasing.

There's so much loss in war – but the last thing I want to lose is my peace of mind.

So, these deaths, although painful, are one hundred per cent necessary.

(January 2019)

Wholeness is a process

'He heals the broken-hearted and binds up their wounds' (Psalms 147:3 NIV).

On heartbreak and healing

Putting all your trust in a dream,

Dissatisfaction and disappointment bruise your self-esteem.

Hope deferred makes the heart sick.

He was only a man.

He could never truly satisfy.

Only a saviour can fill every void your needy soul requires to feel whole.

(March, 2019)

The first step to becoming whole is admitting you require healing.

After the situation with David, I had to face how broken I still was, and admit that I needed God to make me whole. During this time, I went out to eat with one of my friends after church. The tray we were eating on had a beautiful message inscribed on it as part of the restaurant, *Wagamama's* mental health awareness campaign. It was titled *From Broken to Beautiful*. I took a picture of it, but it wasn't until I got home that I read the full text:

Share more than just a meal with a friend

Kintsugi is the Japanese art of mending broken pottery.

Instead of concealing the cracks, gold is used to emphasise the beauty of what was once broken.

The moment we accept and share our struggles is the moment we begin to paint our own cracks with gold.

Wear them with pride as they are a map of a life lived, leaving us stronger and more beautiful than before.

A picture of a black vase with golden cracks immediately came to mind, and I heard the Lord whisper: *This is what I am doing with you.*

'But now, LORD, you are our father. We are the clay, and you are our potter. All of us are the work of your hand.' (Isaiah 64:8 CEB)

The illustration reminded me that, no matter how broken I feel, God can put me back together and create a masterpiece out of my mess.

Process isn't pretty

The truth is the process towards wholeness can be painful. Healing from heartbreak is a crazy journey. One minute you're fine but, reconnect with the person who hurt you, and it becomes apparent that you are still hurting. Distance is needed: healing cannot occur in the environment that made you sick. It takes time to heal, so you must be patient and compassionate towards yourself and realise that God is also patient and compassionate towards you. God cares about us and doesn't enjoy seeing us suffer. As a daughter of God, who you surround yourself with is important. Bad treatment wounds, but people being kind to you brings healing.

'Again, the kingdom of heaven is like a merchant looking for fine pearls. When he found one of great value, he went away and sold everything he had and bought it' (Matthew 13:44-46 NIV).

The above Scripture refers to the value of the Kingdom of Heaven. The same can be said of our worth to God. Imagine Christ Jesus as the merchant, and you are that pearl. He left the glory of heaven to come down to earth to sacrifice his life for us. He became poor so we could have eternal riches; so, you should see yourself as valuable and precious.

When healing from heartbreak, there is no potion you can take or formula that can speed up this process. Only God can heal a broken heart, and he does it in ways we don't expect it. However, I recommend journaling, spending time with your loved ones and creating new experiences. What better way to forget bad memories than by creating new happy ones?

There are different types of love, and God uses different vessels to pour his love into us. During my journey of healing, spending recreational time with friends and family, remind me of just how loved I am. Besides, being single is better than being tied to the wrong person. I know that it doesn't always seem that way, but, remember, not all that glitters is gold.

Knowing our worth doesn't come naturally to most of us. Many grow up with absentee fathers and no male figure to affirm us during our early years, leaving behind wounds that lead us to believe we must look for our worth in men.

I used to believe I didn't have Daddy issues because I knew my dad wanted to be in my life as a child but couldn't because of the situation between him and my mum. I also lived with him during my teenage years; which was more than most of my friends experienced. But as I reflected on certain behavioural traits I have carried into my adulthood, I realised I was wrong. It gets easy to put up a front, but the truth is: even those from nuclear families may have Daddy issues because no biological father is perfect. We all need Jesus to heal us from these wounds.

One of my good friends is called Morenike, which is also one of my middle names. She once told me our name means 'I have found someone to cherish or pamper.' I was so touched. Shouldn't this be the way every woman is treated? Sadly, that is not the case.

We accept the 'love' we think we deserve

Many women fall victim to physical, emotional, psychological, financial or even spiritual abuse, so it's essential to have standards of what we will accept from the men in our lives. I know this is a sensitive topic, but my desire is for you to be free and know that you are worth more than to be beaten up, used or emotionally abused.

A guy I was dating in secondary school once tapped my cheek lightly. It was a slap with no force, so I did the same thing back to him. Before I knew it, I was on the floor, surrounded by his friends who were laughing and mocking me. He had knocked me off my feet, and not in a romantic way. I was so angry and humiliated; I gave him the cold shoulder for a while. I let him know his behaviour was unacceptable, and I wasn't going to put up with it.

'But you hit me first, William.' I said. 'I only hit you back as a joke.'

He wouldn't take responsibility for his actions. 'Yeah, and that was my way of showing you the joke was over.'

William wasn't an aggressive guy, at least not towards me. I think it was meant to show off in front of his friends and try to dominate me. It boils down to immaturity here but just imagine this behaviour on a bigger scale. That should have been enough of a red flag for me to end the relationship and focus on myself and my education. But my feelings for him were clouding my judgement.

Months later, I split up with him for other reasons, but he wouldn't stop phoning me. It was during this time that my friend Matthew reminded me of the incident.

'Ebony, you cannot get back together with him.' He said. 'He floored you, remember? That's so disrespectful.'

I knew it was true, but easier said than done. I genuinely do not think that William would have been a violent partner, had we stayed together, but I deserved better. The treasure inside every woman should not be forgotten. Too often, we compromise and cast our pearls among swine, giving the most valuable parts of ourselves to people who don't deserve us.

Just as a pig will trample on a pearl because it does not understand its value, a man who does not value a virtuous woman will abuse her (Matthew 7:6).

I want to remind you that I am human and still have my struggles, I didn't know I would still be playing *kiss chase* at this age. With my idealistic worldview, I assumed the game would be over by now, and I would be married with children. But, as someone once told me, 'God doesn't work in my time, He works in His', and His timing is perfect.

'When the time is right, I, the Lord, will make it happen' (Isaiah 60:22).

Life is truly a battlefield — you must continuously renew your mind to stay free.

After my first encounter with God at the age of fifteen, I stopped chasing boys for a while. I was so captivated by God's love that He was the only person I wanted to chase. I didn't think I needed a man. If the need isn't there, no desire or void needs filling. But old habits are hard to break.

I've heard people say a woman has already planned her wedding within ten seconds of meeting a guy and I can relate to it in some ways. Not that I plan my entire wedding, but whenever I am interested in a man, my mind skips to marriage. Maybe we've been trained to think that way.

Perhaps I chased boys because no one told me I was the one who was supposed to be pursued. Now that I know that, I've been trying to figure out the best position to be caught by the right man. Like a lady with her eyes fixed firmly on the prize, looking around for the perfect spot to catch the wedding bouquet. I know I'm not alone here.

The Paradox is: this is only part of me. Maybe it's the little girl on the inside, the girl who was abandoned by her Father aged 3, the girl who read herself her own bedtime stories. I think that's the part of me that attached herself to David.

The other part of me, my friends would say, is the equivalent of Margaret Thatcher in the arena of romantic relationships and knows a thing or two about putting up a front. She's a strong, independent, black woman from a line of strong, black women. She tells you she's 'fine, content and happy, and doesn't need a man to complete her' because she genuinely believes only God can do this. Although she doesn't always feel this way, she knows the truth is far greater than her fickle feelings. But this doesn't quench her desire for love, romance, and to have her own family eventually. She was made for love, and it's okay to want what you were made for, right? But her experiences with men have not affirmed the belief that she is, in fact, a queen who deserves the best kind of love from a king.

Trusting God

When Chris Brown released the song *Yo! (Excuse Me, Miss)* in 2005, I was in awe. It spoke to my soul. Here was a song about a guy chasing a girl.

Have you ever been pursued by a guy? How did it make you feel? Loved? Accepted? Special?

Well, that is how God pursues us. *Reckless Love,* a song by Cory Ashbury, talks about God's pursuit. The songwriter states that

'If you don't love me... then I will love me... better yet God will love me.'

— Rachel Kerr

God chases us down, fights for us and leaves ninety-nine of his sheep to find us when we stray. This reflects the parable of the lost sheep in the gospel of Luke and shows us that we are more than a number to God. We must believe we are so valuable to him.

If I put as much energy and effort into my relationship with God as I did chasing boys, would things be different for me? Honestly, what if I was as obsessed with God as I was with Bow Wow, Chris Brown and every other crush since then? What if I put up posters of God's words on my bedroom wall? What if I wrote God a twelve-page long love letter? What if I prayed for the people God cares about? What if I always meditated on and listened to music that glorified Him? I'm sure this would deepen my intimacy with Him. I would feel closer to Him than I usually feel from day-to-day.

But the real question I must ask myself is: *do I trust God*? Can I trust him not to break my heart? Can I trust him not to play games with me and to always be there for me? And why go through all this for someone I can't physically see?

I sometimes struggle to believe he always has my best interests at heart. Not that I think he's bad. I just know that, at times, *I* can be bad, impatient and think I'm entitled, as though a romantic relationship is a reward for good behaviour.

God, can I trust you?

The answer is 'Yes, I can' and here is why.

He is faithful even when we are not. (2 Timothy 2:13)

He is a rewarder of those who diligently seek him. (Hebrews 11:6)

He is a provider. (Genesis 22:14)

His word doesn't return to him empty-handed. (Isaiah 55:11)

Jesus was the fulfilment of a promise God made. (Isaiah 9:6)

He is not a man; therefore, he cannot lie. (Numbers 23:19)

God has promised never to leave or forsake me. (Deuteronomy 31:6 & Hebrews 13:5)

He doesn't change. (Hebrews 13:8)

The Bible is full of testimonies to God's faithfulness, and all the above characteristics assure me that he is entirely trustworthy. These Scriptures remind me that God is in a covenant with me the way a bride and groom enter a marriage covenant. Except, God will not divorce me.

I must also remind myself of the miracles God has done for me in the past.

Chapter 4: Singlehood

'When my soul is in the dumps, I rehearse everything I know of you, From Jordan depths to Hermon heights, including Mount Mizar. Chaos calls to chaos, to the tune of whitewater rapids. Your breaking surf, your thundering breakers crash and crush me. Then GOD promises to love me all day, sing songs all through the night! My life is God's prayer' Psalms 42:6-8 (MSG).

I don't like using the word 'single' because it sounds so lonely. As far as I'm concerned, 'single' doesn't mean 'alone'.

My life has always been my own experience that I've enjoyed so much. I've made great friends, but I also value my time alone with God. I've had the opportunity to do some great things, like pursue my passion for writing, several work opportunities with young people and the public, and the chance to travel to many different places. Besides, even when I was in so-called relationships, I was still single.

There is more to finding your life partner than feeling butterflies. A man and a woman's vision and values must be aligned, and relationships are about sharpening one another and working together to fulfil your God-given assignment. I have never found anyone in whom I see myself; someone who shared the same heart or vision, which goes to show that I am yet to meet the right person.

Not having a romantic partner does not make you incomplete; however, my soul occasionally asks me, 'Why are you **still** single?'

As if *She* has been waiting all her life for this one thing — Marriage.

A happily married woman of God once told me 'your desire for marriage must die before you get married.' I believe she meant your marriage could become an idol if your desire for it has not died in a carnal way. God hates idols, and he will destroy anything that tries to take His place in our hearts.

That's how you can be sure a relationship is from God. If it steals your time with him, you'd better prepare to be separated from that person. If you have more affection for a guy or friend than for Him, God will shake that relationship up because the foundation of every healthy relationship must be Christ. God is a jealous God; he wants us all to himself first before he can give us our life partner. It may seem unreasonable to us, but remember we are his creation and we were made to worship him, not created things.

There is an order to things, and if we step out, we will only reap disorder. That is not what we want, nor what God wants for his children.

Singleness: Gift or Curse?

If we are not careful, we will view singleness as some sort of punishment for sins we committed in the past.

Is singleness a gift? Or is it a punishment? Does it mean I am not yet deserving of the love of a man? If that's the case, I have a lot of work to do. Questions flood my mind like a current, leaving me to wonder and ponder. Sigh.

Another voice whispers to me in a voice that sounds like my own and it says, 'Ebony, what if you never get married? Would you still love and serve God?' *[I recognise that this is fear speaking.]*

Yes, I will, I resolve, and get back to serving.

Perhaps, I should lower my standards, compromise here and there. I mean, he doesn't have to be the best-looking man in the world, but he needs to be godly. That I cannot compromise on.

I could always adopt; my mother was a single mother, and she did it. Another voice speaks as I go about my daily routines, still trying to solve this so-called 'problem.'

I'm strong and independent. I just need to make more money.

This practical voice almost has me convinced. Then I pick up my phone, and while scrolling through Instagram, I notice the striking resemblance between a little girl and her mother.

The maternal part of me begins to whine, *But I want that! I want a mini version of myself!*

God's response to me: *Take delight in me, and I will give you the desires of your heart.*

So, what does it mean to take delight in God? Delighting myself in God means taking pleasure in him. But is God truly enjoyable? Let's look at what the Bible says.

In Psalms 16:11 David says about the Lord: 'You make known to me the path of life; in your presence, there is fullness of joy; at your right hand are pleasures forevermore' (ESV).

I don't know about you, but I experience so much joy and peace when I am in God's presence, and when He speaks to me, it's one-hundred times better than when anyone else does. It soothes my soul, like when you're sick and your mum applies *VapoRub* to your chest. Perhaps that's why they call Him the Balm of Gilead.

I once heard a woman singing to God, and she said, 'in your presence there is ecstasy'. At first, I found this difficult to grasp, because, to be honest, I associate feelings like ecstasy with sexual desires. But God wants us to love him with deep longing, so, this part of her song, I could relate to.

We were made for God's presence, and we cannot live without Him. 'For in Him we live and move and have our being. As some of your own poets have said, 'We are his offspring.' (Acts 17:28 NIV).

The Hebrew word for 'know' in the Bible, *Yada*, describes the most profound way you can know a person. This is the way that Adam knew his wife Eve.

One way we can **yada** God is by believing what the Bible says about him. When we understand that God delights in us, we intrinsically feel closer to him. When the truth that He is *for* us settles in our hearts, it gives us peace. As human social beings, when we know someone likes us, we naturally want to stay connected to them.

The same applies to our relationship with God.

'But I wish everyone were single, just as I am. Yet each person has a special gift from God, of one kind or another. So, I say to those who aren't married and widows — it's better to stay unmarried, just as I am' (1 Corinthians 7:7-8 NLT).

As a teenager, this Bible verse, written by the Apostle Paul, scared my friends and me senseless and was often the topic of discussion at our sleepovers. The primary question was: *What if God wants me to remain single to serve him better?*

We tend to ask more questions when we are younger, but we may not know ourselves well enough to be truly honest about our feelings and emotions.

Back then, we didn't see singleness as a season, but rather a lifelong sentence, depending on what God decided to do with us. This only bred fear, uncertainty and insecurity, which led some of us to make terrible choices. I'm not going to lie to you; it was a huge fear.

The idea of giving up marriage for the greater good sounds honourable, right? Nobody wanted to admit that they would be sorely disappointed if they didn't get married. I think we all just wanted to sound like we were saying the 'right thing' to one another with responses like, 'if it's God's will...so be it'.

As I've matured and gotten to know God better, my beliefs have changed. I don't think God would deny me or anyone who desires to get married this joy here on earth. I believe He gives us our hearts' desires according to His will. That means that He'll give you the best person to marry and confirm whether He sent that person. It's that simple, but we over complicate things. Oh, the woes of being perfectly human!

As a single Christian woman, I cannot stress enough how important it is to plug yourself into a community of believers through attending church, fellowship and Christian events. It may require going out of your way at first, but it will allow you to build relationships vital to your spiritual journey (you must be friendly if you want friends).

Sharing some of my struggles and concerns with fellow sisters in Christ has made me feel better and reminded me that I am not alone. 1 Peter 5:8-10 (NIV) says it best:

'Be alert and of sober mind. Your enemy, the devil prowls around like a roaring lion looking for someone to devour. Resist him, standing firm in the faith, because you know that the family of believers throughout the world is undergoing the same kind of suffering.

*And the God of all grace, who called you to his eternal glory in **Christ**, after you have suffered a little while, will himself restore you and make you strong, firm and steadfast.'*

One of the enemy's most significant lies, when we face a trial or test, is that this is only happening to **you**. He gets us feeling so down about our situations that we believe our case is unusual, and other people are not also trying to overcome similar circumstances. However, the Bible reminds us in 1 Corinthians 10:13 that, 'No temptation has overtaken you except what is common to mankind. And God is faithful; he will not let you be tempted beyond what you can bear. But when you are tempted, he will also provide a way out so that you can endure it' (NIV).

Remaining accountable to others is a good defence weapon. The enemy can only keep deceiving and destroying you if you stay silent about your struggles and do not allow room for wise counsel. This doesn't mean you should speak to everyone – pray for discernment. I recommend speaking to a youth leader, an older person, or a wise friend. Maybe someone who's overcome such situations in the past. They should be someone who keeps confidences.

When building your legacy, it is important to remember: the higher you climb, the greater the fall. Falling from a high position will significantly impact those who look up to you, just as falling from a tall building is more damaging to your body than falling off your chair. Having other Christians to whom you are accountable is vital. When trials and tests come –

and they will – your flesh might resist the truth, but your spirit man will appreciate the wise counsel.

Be aware of red flags. Some relationships are toxic, but we ignore the red flags. When our understanding of our self-worth has been tainted, we believe we deserve the mistreatment we experience. By receiving counsel from those more experienced in walking with the Lord, you'll find it much more difficult to ignore the warning signs, which will ultimately lead to your breakthrough.

Expose whatever darkness you are into the light. It becomes the elephant in the room that can no longer be ignored.

Singleness is time to serve God

'Remember your Creator in the days of your youth, before the days of trouble come and the years approach when you will say, "I find no pleasure in them"' (Ecclesiastes 12:11 NIV).

Being single can be challenging at times. We are conditioned from childhood to idolise relationships with the opposite sex, and we often both subconsciously and consciously chase after the idols and images of 'true love' stored in our minds.

Music videos and movies have been programming and setting us up for disappointment and heartbreak since we were young. Or worse, we enter toxic and abusive relationships based on warped ideas of love and perceptions tainted and influenced by these images.

Most black females who sang love songs when I was growing up were heartbroken. It was normal to suffer on account of a man; cheating was the norm, and it didn't matter how beautiful she was—because 'men are dogs', as I often heard. What's the point in setting standards for relationships if this was the inevitable outcome? Deep down, we know it isn't supposed to be like this.

Ladies, we must divorce lesser ideas of love and hold on to the expectation that there is a man of God out there who will love us like Christ loves the Church (Ephesians 5:25-27).

Lust can be a powerful but damaging emotion. Love is more consistent and patient; it doesn't interrupt or guilt trip you, which might be why it's difficult to recognise. We often take the people who love us for granted because love doesn't expect anything in return. It's not always exciting.

Breaking up with idols

The hardest thing when a relationship ends is breaking up with the mental picture of our future with the person. I've done it many times. With so much uncertainty in life, it's easy to get our hopes up when someone promises us the world. It then becomes tough to accept reality because discontentment rests in our hearts. We may also fear that what we hope for will never happen, especially if we've been waiting a long time.

In moments like this, I like to remind myself of the faith Abraham had.

'When there was no reason for hope, Abraham believed because he had hope. He became the father of many nations, exactly as God had promised. God said, "That is how many children you will have" (Genesis 15:5). Abraham did not become weak in his faith. He accepted the fact that he was past the time when he could have children. At that time Abraham was about 100 years old. He also realized that Sarah was too old to have children. But Abraham kept believing in God's promise. He became strong in his faith. He gave glory to God. He was absolutely sure that God had the power to do what he had promised. That's why "God accepted Abraham because he believed. So his faith made him right with God." (Genesis 15:6) The words "God accepted Abraham's faith" were written not only for Abraham. They were written also for us. We believe in the God who raised Jesus our Lord from the dead. So God will accept our faith and make us right with himself. Jesus was handed over to die for our sins. He was raised to life in order to make us right with God' (Romans 4:18-25 NIRV).

If you read the account of Abraham's life carefully, you will see that he tried to fulfil God's promise to him in his own human ability by sleeping with Hagar, his wife's maidservant, and getting her pregnant with a son. But in the end, we see that God still fulfils his word to him. Abraham could have easily disqualified himself from the promise God made to him after he did this, but instead, he didn't lose faith in God's power and ability.

I hope that encourages you not to give up, as it has also encouraged me.

Like Jesus did, we must relinquish control and submit to the Father's will. And it hurts. I can only imagine what Jesus went through when he headed for the cross.

'Casting down imaginations, and every high thing that exalteth itself against the knowledge of God and bringing into captivity every thought to the obedience of *Christ*' (2 Corinthians 10:5 KJV).

This is part of sharing in his sufferings. We want to experience the glory of being a child of God; we want the resurrection power, but to still have things our way and not experience the pain. But, like the rose and the thorn, sorrow and happiness are linked together.

During times of temptation, I'm reminded that I gave up my rights when I gave my life to Christ. I wasn't saying I would only follow God if he gives me what I want. I was saying 'God, here I am, I need and love you more than life itself, and I'm willing to follow you no matter what comes my way.' I'm bound by the vow I made to God in my heart and at my baptism. (Please read Romans 6:3-7)

'Then, Jesus went to work on his disciples. "Anyone who intends to come with me has to let me lead. You're not in the driver's seat; I am. Don't run from suffering;

> ' For I know the plans *I have for you,*'
> *declares the Lord, 'plans to prosper you*
> *and not to harm you, plans to give you*
> *hope and a future.*'
>
> **Jeremiah 29:11(NIV)**

embrace it. Follow me, and I'll show you how. Self-help is no help at all. Self-sacrifice is the way, my way, to finding yourself, your true self. What kind of deal is it to get everything you want but lose yourself? What could you ever trade your soul for? (Matthew 16:24-26 MSG).

This is a decision I will make again and again until I go home to be with God.

The good news is that God's plan for our lives is far better than the one we have for ourselves—we just need to be patient while his plan unfolds. (Please read Jeremiah 29:11).

Chapter 5: Investing in yourself

For those of us who want to get married. We want to be the best wives and mothers, and still be good friends, sisters and daughters. However, the strength of any relationship is in the strength of the individuals, so your marriage preparation should begin now.

Everyone knows something that will last must have a strong foundation. I believe it is vital for anyone who desires to get married to have a strong foundation in God's word.

The wait can be challenging, but it's important not to rush down the altar. There are many divorced 30-year olds. I don't know about you, but I want a marriage that will endure a lifetime, not barely scrape a decade.

The more I learn about godly principles for marriage, the more I understand that it is no light matter. I'd rather wait longer and have a lasting marriage, than rush into things with the wrong person at the wrong time or even with the right person at the wrong time.

In the book of Ecclesiastes 7:8, the Bible teaches us that **patience is better than pride**. If your sole purpose for getting married is to show off to others or tick the 'married by 30' box, you might have to re-evaluate your motivation. God is far too kind to give us responsibilities we cannot handle.

Be patient! Your time is coming! (I'm preaching to myself).

To build a solid foundation for the future we desire, we must become the best version of ourselves right now.

At twenty-six, I began to understand the importance of investing in myself spiritually, physically and mentally. A high-value woman needs to know how to 'mind her own business', which means she must stay committed to her growth and progress in life.

A high-value woman is responsible for her life and happiness, and she makes things happen through her everyday choices. In other words, she's a Girl Boss and go-getter who makes no apologies for who she is. Because she knows that even the most amazing of men have their weaknesses, she's not waiting for Prince Charming. She is focused on becoming whole and fulfilling her God-given assignment.

My friend Esther Jacob posted this on her WhatsApp status from 1 Thessalonians 4:11.

Take these five skills into account:

1. To lead and live a quiet life

2. To mind your own business

3. To work with your hands

4. To influence outsiders

5. To depend on nobody

I was blown away when I read this. The Bible gives us so much practical advice. All the points here are vital to living successfully on earth. Let's take the time to expand on each one.

To lead and live a quiet life

Ever heard the saying 'empty vessels make the most noise'? I am an expressive person, so I like to post on social media as an outlet. I wouldn't say I've mastered it, but sometimes I just need to step back and be quiet, especially when I am in a season of building. I work best in silence because that is when I can hear God instruct me on what to do next; which may mean taking a break from social media from time to time. While it can be an excellent tool for promoting businesses, connecting with and ministering to others, social media can also become an idol and a distraction. We can use it to fill up time and feed our egos, which, of course, is not pleasing to God.

I must also consider whether my post glorifies God or myself; or if it even edifies others. I admit I sometimes find this challenging, but when the Holy Spirit tells me to remove a post or picture, I try to obey Him quickly. It is important to step back from the things that can distract us from God and destroy our souls.

Living a quiet life can also mean living peacefully with others. I don't like to reveal too much about myself when I enter a new environment. I take my time to study the surroundings and company I am in. Some may think I'm shy, but, most of the time, I'm just quietly observing. Talking too much, especially to the wrong people, can get you in a lot of trouble and do more damage than staying silent.

To mind your own business

We have been taught that minding your own business means to stay out of other people's affairs. While this is true, it also means to focus on your own life. Gossip is a harmful waste of time. I rarely enjoy talking about people who do not concern me, like celebrities, for instance. I engaged in gossip a lot when I was younger, but now that I know better, I find myself having fewer of these types of conversations. I recognise that, as social beings, we like to converse, so if someone brings up a person, I try to understand where they are coming from and give insight. It works well to be kind.

Focusing on your own life is a powerful skill that empowers you. It can seem selfish to others, but minding your own business is a real strength. It requires self-discipline (which many of us lack) because it causes you to focus on yourself. You can't find your purpose when focusing on others, and it only highlights your insecurity if you're unsure of where you're going. However, minding my own business and understanding my assignment made me realise that I bring something unique to the table. It enables me to also see others as sources of inspiration, rather than objects of envy which is rooted in insecurity.

To work hard with your hands

One must never forget the importance of hard work and its benefits in this microwave, Instagram generation where everyone wants quick results. Everything takes time and effort; nothing happens without action and, although it may seem that way when you're looking at others, success doesn't happen overnight.

I'm a firm believer that God will openly reward what you do in secret. Many people can assume your accomplishments came easily, but social media doesn't show them the groundwork you put in behind the scenes. You cannot see a seed planted in soil because the roots go down before the shoot goes up. Only lazy and immature people want success with no process.

Whatever you do, do your best. Don't focus on anyone else.

To influence outsiders

Everyone was created to be established. The Christian's role is to model Christ to a broken world. The Bible says **you will know them by their fruits** (Matthew 7:16 NKJV). People watch our lives, and we influence them whether we realise it or not. After I first left my tutoring job, a young man messaged me to say my being rooted in Christ helped him, especially at work. I had no idea I was a positive influence on him.

Many people will never tell you how you inspire or influence them but, trust me, you do!

To depend on nobody

I think this final point is so crucial to becoming a high-value woman. It's important to stand on your own feet. Be dependent on God, but it is unwise to depend on people. Disappointments have taught me that everyone I trust will let me down at some point, and vice versa. I may even let myself down. I have close friends, but Jesus is my best friend.

You can develop your skills because you have great potential, but you need first to believe and work on it!

Ways I choose to invest in myself are by reading books and listening to podcasts on faith, finances and personal development. I am prepared to pay the price to become the woman I have always dreamed of becoming – independent of my marital status.

Are you?

It's hard work that must be done.

Chapter 6: God's wife

During my final year at university, I lived with a lady called Caroline. She was an international student from China who was full of wisecracks. We got along very well because she loved to make jokes, and I love to laugh. One night I allowed her to sleep in my room because she had misplaced her key and couldn't get back into hers.

'I'm just going to pray for us, if that's ok.' I said.

She agreed.

'Amen,' she said after I said a short prayer. 'Ebony, you are so nice. You are a Christian who actually believes.'

If only she knew my struggle.

I was working late in the library one evening when I noticed her sitting at a computer.

'Hi, Carol,' I said as I passed by.

'Oh, hey, Ebony.' Startled, she peered at me through her glasses, noticing the jumper I was wearing. She read it aloud, 'First...Love...Church.'

I looked down and giggled. I'd forgotten I was wearing it.

'You are God's wife.'

Carol wasn't a Christian, so her statement took me by surprise. I laughed and continued to make small talk. Once we parted ways, I kept thinking about what she had said.

You are God's wife.

Carol had no idea how on the ball she was. I was God's wife but hadn't known it. Earlier that year, God had shown me a book in a dream. The book opened and, as if someone was reading it to me, an audible voice said, 'THOU SHALL NOT FORNICATE. THOU SHALL NOT COMMIT ADULTERY.'

I woke up and tried to make sense of the dream. I understood why the Lord would send me a warning against fornication. At the time, I was going into a relationship with a non-Christian; and the Lord disciplines those he loves. The line about adultery puzzled me though. I understand that adultery doesn't have to be physical. Here's what Jesus says about it in Matthew 5:27-28 (NIV): 'You have heard that it was said, "You shall not commit adultery." But I tell you that anyone who looks at a woman lustfully has already committed adultery with her in his heart.'

Adultery. How could I commit adultery if I'm not married?

But I was. I was married to God and being unfaithful to him. 'For your Maker is your husband-the LORD Almighty is his name- the Holy One of Israel is your Redeemer; he is called the God of all the earth' (Isaiah 54:5 NIV).

If you're like me, you might find this concept difficult to fathom. *How can God be your husband?*

Oh, but He is. He loves, cares for and cherishes you. He provides for, protects, and is 100% committed to you. All these qualities make him the perfect husband. When Jesus died on the Cross, he was extending an invitation – let's call it a proposal – to us all. When we believed, repented, and were baptised, we accepted his offer and entered a covenant with him.

The Church is described in the Bible as 'the bride of Christ'. We put so much emphasis on marriage here on earth—too much—when, in heaven, we will all be married to God, for eternity.

Just think about it if you want to get married one day. If you cannot submit to God now, how will you submit to your earthly husband when you get married? We rarely see the bigger picture when God is disciplining us. However, the Bible teaches us that God disciplines us for our good so we can share in his holiness.

In the Greek language, 'to worship' means 'to kiss'. Remember what I wrote at the beginning about kiss chase? Well, it's time we stopped chasing boys and started playing kiss chase with the only One who truly satisfies.

Fall in Love with God all over again

I once heard a lady say she fell in love with God as she read the following Bible verses, so I needed to read them for myself.

'This is what the Sovereign Lord says to Jerusalem: "Your ancestry and birth were in the land of the Canaanites; your father was an Amorite and your mother, a Hittite. On the day you were born, your cord was not cut, nor were you washed with water to make you clean, nor were you rubbed with salt or wrapped in cloths. No one looked on you with pity or had compassion enough to do any of these things for you. Rather, you were thrown out into the open field, for on the day you were born you were despised.

"Then I passed by and saw you kicking about in your blood, and as you lay there in your blood, I said to you, 'Live!' I made you grow like a plant of the field. You grew and developed and entered puberty. Your breasts had formed, and your hair had grown, yet you were stark naked.

"Later I passed by, and when I looked at you and saw that you were old enough for love, I spread the corner of my garment over you and covered your naked body. I gave you my solemn oath and entered into a covenant with you," declares the Sovereign Lord, "and you became mine"' (Ezekiel 16:3-8 NIV.)

God is a passionate God. This passage of Scripture reminds me of when I first experienced the love of God and received the Holy Spirit. God almighty covered me with his perfect love at a time when I felt vulnerable. I'd never felt so complete in my entire life.

God is my husband, but if I'm honest, I haven't been the best wife.

What kind of wife are you to God?

Are you a contentious wife?

'An endless dripping on a rainy day and a nagging wife are alike' (Proverbs 27:15 CSB).

God wants us to ask him for things, but there is a difference between making requests and nagging. Do you spend most of your quality time with God complaining or giving thanks? This largely indicates whether you are a contentious wife. No husband wants a wife who is always argumentative and complaining about how he can do better. The same is true of our relationship with God. God responds well to praise and thanksgiving. I believe he multiplies anything you are thankful for in your life.

Are you a busy wife?

The book of Luke tells the story of two sisters, Martha and Mary, who welcomed Jesus into their home. Martha was so busy serving the Lord that she had no time to spend with him. I can just picture her rushing around the house busily preparing his room and what He would eat. Whereas Mary was in the living room, happily sitting at his feet.

Martha became upset that she was doing all the housework while Mary was resting. Here's what the Lord had to say to Martha after she lashed out at him.

'Martha, Martha,' The Lord answered, 'you are worried and upset about many things, but few things are needed- or indeed only *one*. Mary has chosen what is better, and it will not be taken away from her.' (Luke 10:41-42 NIV).

The same is true for us; it is better to spend quality time with the Lord than allow ourselves to get worked up about our assignment.

The greatest commandment God gives us is to love him with all our heart, strength, soul and mind. This must come first. That's why the Bible also teaches us that without love, we are nothing.

I'm learning the difference between my purpose and my assignment. My purpose is to love, worship and spend time with God, and part of my assignment and service to him is to write books. I cannot do the latter if I neglect the first – it would be meaningless.

'Remain in me, as I also remain in you. No branch can bear fruit by itself; it must remain in the vine. Neither can you bear fruit unless you remain in me.' (John 15:4 NIV).

God wants us to have fruitful, not busy lives. There's a difference: we can only bear fruit if we abide in him.

Are you a promiscuous and adulterous wife?

In Hosea 1:2, God tells the prophet Hosea to marry a prostitute called Gomer, to mirror his relationship with the nation of Israel. Can you imagine how distressing it would be to be married to someone who is always cheating on you?

If we're sincere, we sometimes fall into all those different categories.

But what kind of wife does God want?

'Who can find **a virtuous wife**? For her worth is far above rubies. The heart of her husband safely trusts her; So, he will have no lack of gain. (Proverbs 31:10-11 NKJV)

To be virtuous means to have or show high moral standards. This is the type of wife we all need to strive to be.

I visited my Dad's hometown in Nigeria for the first time in March 2018. One of the trip's highlights was meeting my older female cousin, Tope (I called her Aunty Tope out of respect). She was married to a Pastor and told me she sensed God was calling me into ministry.

'That sounds about right,' I replied, reflecting on my life experiences. There wasn't a doubt in my mind that this was true.

While in Nigeria, I woke up early one morning and felt led to study the Proverbs 31 woman. Here's what I discovered about this woman:

She is worth more than diamonds. Her husband can trust, rely and depend on her as an asset, not a liability. She is hardworking and resourceful, a provider for her household, and a disciplined morning bird. She always puts her family first and thinks about the needs of others. She has her own income, is intelligent, and spiritually and physically strong. She is a skilful and proactive humanitarian and, when she speaks, wisdom flows.

Coincidentally, a few days later, Aunty Tope informed me that my dad had asked her to speak on his radio station. The topic she had chosen was 'The Virtuous Woman' from Proverbs 31.

She asked me to join her, and we ended up streaming a live video later that afternoon. On the Livestream, I gave my opinion of a virtuous woman from a single woman's perspective. From a married woman's perspective, Aunty Tope stated that the dictionary definition of virtue was morally good behaviour or character. She was a woman of distinction, grace and excellence. I learned a lot from this discussion.

Eight months later, after my first book launch, a young man messaged to tell me I was *virtuous*. It was the nicest thing a man had ever said to me.

Virtuous? Me? I knew this young man had read my book, so I was humbled that he knew the worst about me but still saw the best in me.

Isn't that how God treats us?

It also made me wonder: *what virtuous attributes had I adopted?*

True Intimacy

Intimacy with God is better than intimacy with anybody else but spending time alone with him is not always easy. It can leave you feeling vulnerable because you can't hide anything from him – but it's necessary. Sometimes, I think I like the idea of spending time with God more than the actual practice. His presence highlights my brokenness and need for a saviour and healing.

Below is a poem the Lord gave me one evening on the bus home from work:

Intimacy: Into me you see

You talk about intimacy like you don't know what it is, yet you have it all the time.
You are intimate with your friends.

Intimacy is birthed from trust.
You want to be intimate with me, yet you don't trust me.
There can be no intimacy without relationship, so, are you ready?
Are you ready to let me in?
Are you ready to open your heart?
Are you ready to tell me your deepest fears?
Are you ready to listen to my advice?
Are you ready for true, deep, personal intimacy?
Are you ready to be refined by love?
Are you ready to allow my love to change you?
To heal, discipline and transform you?

Do you know your maker?
Do you want to know who I am?
Do you want me to tell you what's on my mind?
Are you ready?
Do you want to know me...?

Because, just like you, I long to be known.
Just like you… I long to be understood, heard and
appreciated.
Just like you, I wonder: will my people ever accept me?
Will I be enough?
I am enough, but will I be enough for them?
Will they get bored with me?
Will they be dissatisfied with me?

I have so much I want to show you, but are you ready?
I know you can't comprehend your capacity for such
love and intimacy,
but I manufactured you, so I know what you're made of.

It's my image you bear.
It's the image of my son
Written on your heart.
(23 March 2019)

'This is what the Lord says: 'What fault did your ancestors find in me, that they strayed so far from me? They followed worthless idols and became worthless themselves' (Jeremiah 2:5 NIV).

Building intimacy with God can be done in a variety of ways. One way I've done this over the years is through journaling. I write out my prayers and thoughts of gratitude and tell him my deepest concerns. I find that I feel closest to him when I sing worship songs to him, I can sense his delight and I am equally as delighted because the Holy Spirit lives in me, I'm filled with joy.

A time when my faith grew significantly was back in 2016. I attended a church that encouraged daily quiet times, so I would read a passage of scripture in the morning and shared my notes with a friend. It revolutionised my life. The consistent time and effort I spend reading the scriptures to develop my understanding have been the key to stability in my walk with Christ. During certain seasons, I express my emotions by reading passages of scripture aloud while lying in bed. You should try it; it is so refreshing; I recommend reading Psalms 42 in The Message or The Passion Translation.

I still struggle to spend alone time with God. When I don't, I feel him calling me back to the 'secret chamber' as I like to call it. I can be stubborn at times, but in that secret place, I can be 100% honest. That is where real intimacy and trust is built.

Be a virtuous wife to God first. Love and serve Him with your whole heart.

Submission and Service

We all have an assignment to fulfil on this earth. Whether you're an usher in your church, a public speaker, or both, you've been called to serve the body of Christ, lead God's lost sheep home and lead unbelievers to Christ. The main thing is to do it as unto God and not man. He sees everything you are doing and will reward you – when the time is right.

Your First Love

'To the angel of the church in Ephesus write: "The words of him who holds the seven stars in his right hand, who walks among the seven golden lampstands. "I know your works, your toil and your patient endurance, and how you cannot bear with those who are evil but have tested those who call themselves apostles and are not and found them to be false. I know you are enduring patiently and bearing up for my name's sake, and you have not grown weary. But I have this against you, that you have abandoned the love you had at first. Remember, therefore, from where you have fallen; repent, and do the works you did at first."' (Revelation 2:1-5 ESV).

Beloved, bride of Christ, do you remember your first crush? The first guy who ever made your heartbeat so fast that you thought it would fly out of your chest. God wants us to feel this way about Him. In the book of Revelation, God ends up telling a church to repent and turn back to their first love.

'Be zealous and repent, return to your first love' (Revelation 3:19 ESV). To be zealous means to show the same level of eagerness and enthusiasm you did at first.

To understand how we can return to God, our first love, I asked a couple who had been married for seven years how they return to the moments when they first fell in love. I was fascinated when Vanessa said she was now more in love with her husband than when they got together. Her husband, Zory, said love was a decision. Some of their tips included:

1. Growing in love—learning to depend on one another.
2. Building love—not wanting to jeopardise the love they'd built.
3. Maintaining eye contact—when having difficult conversations.

Vanessa and Zory explained their view that many relationship problems stem from people entering marriages or, partnerships with expectations or heartbreak from a previous relationship, which start sprouting as insecurities and fears within them.

'When some people become Christians, they create these fairy-tale expectations of God. When things are not as rosy, they end up drifting off.' Vanessa said.

I realised how I projected my past heartbreaks and disappointments onto God and how this affects my relationship with him. That's why Christians must know the unchanging character of God.

The main takeaway from my discussion with Vanessa and Zory was their commitment to stand by each other through thick and thin. They made me understand that **first love** isn't purely based on emotions but rather the commitment they've made to choose to love one another.

Chapter 7: Self-love, Self-worth and Value

We live in a generation that preaches about self-love, not only in the secular world but in our churches. It is taught everywhere. The idea is to love yourself because, if you do, you won't let others mistreat you. Love yourself, and you can love others better. You should also love yourself and care for your physical appearance. Although this is true, I would like to share some thoughts on the topic.

I've heard people ask: 'How do you expect others to love you if you don't love yourself?'

Whilst I believe the way you carry yourself is important – I think the beautiful thing about the gospel is in John 3:16 (NIV): 'For God so loved the world, that he gave his only begotten Son, that whosoever believes in him should not perish, but have everlasting life.'

When Jesus died on the cross for our sins, he restored value that had been stolen, through idolatry, to man.

> 'But you are a chosen people, a royal priesthood, a holy nation, God's special possession, that you may declare the praises of him who called you out of darkness into his wonderful light. Once you were not a people, but now you are the people of God; once you had not received mercy, but now you have received mercy' (1 Peter 2:9-10 NIV).

It's comforting to realise how much God loves us despite our fallen human nature. God has used many people to love me despite my not completely loving myself. My actions and poor choices were proof that I was not only struggling to recognise my worth, but I was also falling short of God's standard. I think the song, *Lovin' Me*, by Jonathan McReynolds,[4] describes this perfectly.

Let me explain how the Bible talks about these last days:

> 'For men will be lovers of themselves, lovers of money, boasters, proud, blasphemers, disobedient to parents, unthankful, unholy' (2 Timothy 3:2 BSB).

> 'For the world offers only a craving for physical pleasure, a craving for everything we see, and pride in our achievements and possessions. These are not from the Father but are from this world' (1 John 2:16 NLT).

Much of modern culture is fuelled by selfishness and egocentrism. If we love the things of the world, we cannot love God. The key is to use them as tools—not let them use you. Money is a by-product of using your skills to serve others.

The Bible also tells us we have value in Christ. Years ago, I was having a hard time with my faith after being discharged from the mental health hospital. I was in church one day when Ian, my church's youth

---

[4] https://www.youtube.com/watch?v=mfyVeJ2OdQg

leader, told me something about me was special to God.

I had no idea what he was talking about. I was under such condemnation; I felt I didn't deserve to hear those words. I'd heard them so many times before, but they still hadn't sunk in. I had expected Ian to rebuke me, but I received the opposite: affirmation, love and concern.

Years later, I sat down with him over a meal at Nando's.

'I feel like I'm not doing enough.' I said.

'Hmm...' He chewed his chicken slowly. 'Something not fulfilling its potential doesn't mean it's any less valuable.'

I stopped eating to concentrate on the wisdom I knew he would provide. 'How do you mean?'

'Let's take a potato, for example. You can bake it, roast, or even fry it like these chips, but that potato in its raw form is just as valuable.'

'That's true.' Conversations with Ian always left me pondering.

The problem is that some people don't understand the difference between being narcissistic and knowing your worth and value.

Some things can only be understood from a manufacturer's perspective. Let's say you, a product manufactured by God, have malfunctioned. Should your manufacturer throw you away? No, he will work on fixing you until you function the way you are supposed to. Why? Because God not only took his time in creating you.

The price people are willing to pay for an item represents its worth. God thought we were valuable enough to die for. He demonstrated that we were worth redeeming when he sent Jesus into the world to die for us. God

demonstrated that we were worth redeeming by sending Jesus into the world to die for us before we even made a single mistake. Even before we knew of God and could worship him. We tend to show more grace to others, especially new believers in the faith, than to ourselves. But God, in his kindness, extends the same mercy to us all.

Love yourself

As a Christian, you're not taught to love yourself, but to put others before yourself; to love even your enemies. This is true, but I've come to understand that self-love isn't selfish or wrong. I'm not talking about the narcissistic kind of self-love but believing you are worthy and valuable.

When you begin to believe you have inherent, intrinsic, infinite value, it causes you to be less tolerant of anything that tries to undermine these truths.

Here is a poem I wrote about myself when I was feeling low.

Worthy

I'm worth love and affection.

I know I'm worth it.

I'm worth someone paying attention to every detail of my face.

I know I'm worth it.

I'm worth your reply.

I know I'm worth it.

I'm worth your time.

I know I'm worth it.

I'm worth your love.

I know I'm worth it.

I'm worth the apology.

I know I'm worth it.

I'm worth the pursuit.

I know I'm worth it.

I'm worth the chase.

I know I'm worth it.

I'm worth the fear that you feel when you think about losing me.

I sure am worth it.

I'm worth the anger you feel when you see me with another guy.

I know I'm worth it.

I'm worth the Facebook and Instagram likes.

I sure am worth it.

I'm worth it. I'm worth it. I am worth it.

(December 2018)

On inner beauty, gentleness and quiet confidence

'Your beauty should not come from outward adornment, such as elaborate hairstyles and the wearing of gold jewellery or fine clothes. Rather, it should be that of your inner self, the unfading beauty of a gentle and quiet spirit, which is of great worth in God's sight (1 Peter 3:3-4 NIV).'

Cultivate inner beauty, it is precious to God. I don't think there's ever been a time in history where women have not been concerned about their looks. We all have insecurities, but your insecurities should not have you! Your physical appearance is important, but how you are inside is even more so. As God's daughters, we need to remember this because Instagram may have some of us fooled. People seem to allow the world, rather than God's word, to define their standards of beauty. How heart-breaking it must be for the Father to see his creation having an identity crisis and be unable to step in because we won't allow Him.

You lose your physical beauty as you get older. That's why it's better to have a godly character, not just beauty (Proverbs 31:30 AMP). I'm not against physical adornment; if you can have both, great! It takes a lot of time, effort and self-discipline to stay fit, look good and still serve God. I admire women who do so; in fact, I want to be one of them! Just remember: the outward appearance is temporary, but the internal is eternal, so make that your priority!

I believe God will help us with this because getting the balance right is essential.

Do not lose sight of the fact that you are God's favourite – you are his masterpiece.

'For we are God's masterpiece. He has created us anew in Christ Jesus, so we can do the good things he planned for us long ago (Ephesians 3:10 NLT).'

In October 2019, at a conference I attended abroad, the famous, influential motivational speaker Les Brown said, 'you are God's masterpiece because you are a piece of the Master.' That hit me.

We often see ourselves as insignificant and small, but the more I walk with God, the more I understand that he thinks very highly of human beings. We were created in The Most Supreme being's image and likeness. Knowing this should give us immense confidence.

The higher your value, the bigger your impact.

You don't have to be the loudest person in the room to make the most impact. You simply need to make your voice heard, and your message understood. I am not a naturally loud person; my voice is gentle and quiet, but when I speak, my words carry power and authority. And I know I have a message to share.

God hides his treasure in jars of clay

I never pictured myself as a public speaker; not even in 2017 when I participated in the Beauty and Creativity pageant, Miss E.B.O.N.Y. Ambassador. I was nervous about public speaking, but it was an area I wanted to develop in.

I suppose my dread of public speaking stemmed from my secondary school days where we were critical of one another in the name of banter. One wrong sentence, or even a stutter, and you became the joke for the rest of the day or week. Although it was fun to laugh at others, I developed a fear of being mocked.

I do recall a day at school when my English teacher, Mr Straker, asked me to read a passage aloud from a book we were studying in class.

'You read well.' He commented after I had finished. It boosted my confidence.

Today, my confidence grows the more I speak. It is as though I'm building my speaking muscles and I am still growing in the gift. However, when I watch videos from events I've spoken at, I almost don't recognise myself because I look more confident than I felt at the time!

The importance of introspection, meditation and reflection

The moment we stop exercising our gifts and talents, we lose ourselves.

Spending time on your own for personal development is valuable. This requires focus and discipline—you must minimise distractions. Humans need structure and when we don't have it, we feel lost and afraid. A successful life requires a lot of hard work and discipline. Just like you must watch what you eat and motivate yourself to work out to stay physically fit; focus, hard work, and discipline yield amazing results.

The art of being yourself

Don't chase love. Become love, and you will attract what you have become.

Now that I know what love is, I am content with just being.

The need for external things to fill the God-shaped void in my soul slowly starts to lose its grip.

As I cultivate the earth inside of me — my heart — I allow love to grow and mature.

As I spend time hidden under the shadow of the Almighty, abiding in God who is love, this thought becomes clearer.

I am no longer just experiencing love – I am becoming LOVE.

(February 2019)

'As a man thinketh, so is He' (Proverbs 23:7 KJV)

It all begins with you.

My good friend Arnold gave me some advice when I began my journey as an author that I'd like to share with you.

1. Be yourself and the right people and opportunities will be attracted to you.
2. Continue to do what you love.
3. Continue to develop yourself.
4. Don't look for love: love yourself, and people will love you.
5. Don't look for acceptance: accept yourself, and people will accept you.'

I began to think about how many people think they have problems with other people.

Many fail to recognise that the real problem they have is not with others but themselves.

They feel people don't value them. They don't value themselves.

They feel people have abandoned them. They have given up on themselves.

They feel people are not there for them. They don't believe they have what it takes to make it themselves.

They are unhappy with others. They haven't taken the time to realise what truly makes them happy.

- People are looking for hope—become Hope.
- People are looking for light—become Light.
- People are looking for inspiration—become Inspiration.
- People are looking for love—become Love.

Then you will attract people to you and win souls for Christ.

Emotional intelligence

Have you ever thought that God has emotions, but they do not bind him? We were made in his image, but how many of us are bound by our feelings? We're not robots, but we must give God's word supremacy. Ultimately, our character matters the most.

I once watched a Ted Talk in which the lady spoke about how to be in tune with our emotions but not let them rule us. She described emotions as indicators. For example, sadness is a sign that something is wrong. Jealousy can be a sign that we are supposed to do something we haven't yet done. You might feel jealous that someone has released a book, or they have a successful relationship or marriage. Because you don't believe you're capable or entitled to these good things you desire, you feel envious.

What you need to work and focus on is your faith, not the other person. It is better to look internally at the root cause rather than projecting those insecurities on another person.

Let's read what God has to say about this issue:

'What causes fights and quarrels among you? Don't they come from your desires that battle within you? You desire but do not have, so you kill. You covet, but you cannot get what you want, so you quarrel and fight. You do not have because you do not ask God. When you ask, you do not receive, because you ask with wrong motives, that you may spend what you get on your pleasures.

'You adulterous people, don't you know that friendship with the world means enmity against God? Therefore, anyone who chooses to be a friend of the world becomes an enemy of

112

God. Or do you think Scripture says without reason that he jealously longs for the spirit he has caused to dwell in us? But he gives us more grace. That is why Scripture says: 'God opposes the proud but shows favour to the humble.'

'Submit yourselves, then, to God. Resist the devil, and he will flee from you. Come near to God, and he will come near to you. Wash your hands, you sinners, and purify your hearts, you double-minded. Grieve, mourn and wail. Change your laughter to mourning and your joy to gloom. Humble yourselves before the Lord, and he will lift you up (James 4:1-10 NIV).'

God is not a respecter of persons – he responds to faith. Any fear-rooted envy begins to disappear once you realise that what you desire is attainable.

'Whatever your hand finds to do... do it with all your heart (Ecclesiastes 9:10).' You cannot do everything but do whatever you can well! Remember, only you can do what you do the way you do it.

Tips for overcoming comparison and feelings of failure

1. Stay focused and committed to your goals.

2. Remind yourself that success doesn't happen overnight.

3. Celebrate your previous accomplishments, no matter how small.

113

4. Be grateful for your life – Your achievements do not determine your worth and value.

5. Do not be too hard on yourself.

6. Remember, everyone's journey is different.

7. Start looking to God, not people, for validation.

We live in a generation that seeks validation from social media. It's so easy to get caught up in the hype, do not forget you are in the world but not of it.

Let God validate you

Everyone wants to be validated. We want to feel special, valuable and unique; and to be recognised for our talents and gifts. But many people have self-doubt. I must stress that your validation should not come from people because when they (inevitably) let you down, how will you overcome it?

Words of affirmation are one of my love languages, and I love to share things with those closest to me. But what happens when my friend or family member doesn't like my social media post, or they no longer encourage me like they used to? Or forget to wish me a happy birthday... or I don't get the reaction I expect when I tell them my good news? I've experienced all the above, and it hurts. Will I break down? Will I stop believing in myself because they haven't validated me? Certainly not, because that gives people too much power over me, and I must learn not to if I want to go far in life.

Hearing the words: 'Well done, my good and faithful servant! You have been faithful in handling this small amount, so now I will give you many more responsibilities. Let's celebrate together (Matthew 25:21 NLT)' should be all the validation you need.

I encourage you to make this your mission in life. This mindset will shift you from complacency to productivity and change your focus to impressing God, not people, which leads to my next point.

8. Trust that God is a rewarder of those who diligently seek him.

Chapter 8: Lessons from seasons past

Arise, shine, for your light has come, and the glory of the LORD rises upon you (Isaiah 60:1 NIV).

Life isn't always going to be roses and sunshine; there will be low periods. In those times, we must learn to encourage ourselves. Below are some poems I have written during some of my most difficult moments. I hope they help you see that you are not alone, and things will get better.

'My God turns my darkness into light' (Psalms 18:28 NIV)

Gloomy day

Oh, gloomy day

The sun will rise tomorrow

And lift this dark cloud from over my head

I said the Son will arise tomorrow

The Son WILL arise tomorrow

Hope will arise tomorrow

New joy, new strength will arise tomorrow

I will arise tomorrow with more wisdom, more understanding, more joy and more grace in Jesus' name.

Gloomy day

I will forsake all my pain on this gloomy day

I'll pray it all away

On this gloomy day

I will abandon every foreign god on this gloomy day.

I'll remove every foreigner from my house on this gloomy day.

I'll abandon my fear and shame on this gloomy day.

I'll let the light overtake me on this gloomy night.

For I know that his light will shine bright over my gloomy nights

No more gloomy days.

(May 2015)

Notice how my gloomy day became a gloomy night; demonstrating just how long we can dwell in a dark place when we go through a challenging circumstance. But it also shows that time passes, and seasons change.

I wrote the poem after a breakup. I hope it encourages you to find a way to articulate whatever you are going through so that when you look back, you can see how far you've come.

The woman you are becoming will cost you people, relationships, spaces and material things. Choose her over everything!

Knowing your worth means you will have to say 'no' to people and things that no longer serve you.

It's hard changing from people-pleasing to a God-pleaser because it requires saying no to people and opportunities that do not align with your purpose. If you're someone who gets your validation from what others think of you, you will find this problematic.

In 2001, Britney Spears wrote a song called 'I'm a slave for you' that I sang along to as a little girl. Looking back at the song lyrics, I can see how women are conditioned to please men. But there's a difference between serving others in love and being their slave.

Are you a slave?

Oxford Languages defines slavery as 'a condition of having to work very hard without proper remuneration or appreciation.'

Do you feel like you are working overtime to please someone? You may have become their slave. We people-please because we are scared. We do not want them to think negatively towards us and, in turn, we don't want to feel bad about ourselves. Fear makes us slaves, but love makes us servants.

Setting boundaries is the only way to stop people from taking advantage of you. People may not always like it, but, in the long run, they'll learn to accept it and prove whether they genuinely respect you.

I remember a time when I found myself drawn towards an attractive bad boy who quickly opened up to me about his promiscuous past. As I listened to what he said, I thought *this man does not love himself, or he would realise that sexual impurity* **degrades the body.** He did not value or see his body as something sacred. How could someone like that honour me and my body? Honouring your body is the best form of self-care.

It made me sad because I knew that, no matter what I did, I couldn't change him. Fundamentally, he was broken inside. That's when I realised that love must be applied with wisdom.

I don't know why some of us women develop a 'saviour complex' and think we are powerful enough to change a man. We believe we can fix and heal him. That, somehow, we are enough. You're not responsible for another person's healing, but you are responsible for yours.

As tough as it is, we must let go of unhealthy friendships and relationships in order to heal. A wound cannot heal if it is continuously being infected. If someone in your life causes more pain than joy, you've got to find a way to let them go. Don't allow compassion to blind you, just because you're trying to be a good Christian. You'll be fine and so will they. It will all work out in the end.

I've always been the type of person who loves **hard.** You could say I wear my heart on my sleeve, but I'm learning that to love without applying wisdom is foolish. Wisdom will help you discern how to best love someone (Proverbs 19:8 NLT). And that, sometimes, means walking away.

Learn to care about other people without taking on all their problems. Other people's problems are not your responsibility.

I get it, we want to help others, and we should, but there must be a balance. If I learned anything from my mental health breakdown, it is that I am not Jesus— only he can manage the world on his shoulders. I will do everything I can do to support you, but the best person I can recommend to you is God.

Even as a mentor or role model, I do not want to mislead people. I am human, and therefore, fallible. If you put me on a pedestal, you will be disappointed, but if you hold God to a high standard, you will never be disappointed. No one, absolutely no one, should take God's place in your heart.

Heartbeats

My heart no longer beats the way it used to.

It has a new rhythm. It no longer beats for you.

She learned that she could not serve two masters and so she found a new rhythm.

It was a rhythm unfamiliar to her at first, but one that would become her own.

A new anthem.

With every breath, a new lullaby; with every pump, a new flow.

I tell you the truth.

My heart no longer beats the way it used to - it no longer beats for you.

(July 2019)

God loves us too much to leave us in toxic relationships where we are devalued.

The Secret Chambers of the heart

Guard your heart - everything you do flows from it (Proverbs 24:3).

A chamber is a private place, like a bedroom, into which no one can see but God. I asked at the beginning of this book: who or what is sitting on the throne of your heart?

The heart has four chambers: two atria and two ventricles. **The right atrium** receives oxygen-poor blood from the **body** and pumps it to the **right ventricle**. The **right ventricle** pumps the oxygen-poor blood to the **lungs**. The **left atrium** receives oxygen-rich blood from the **lungs** and pumps it to the **left ventricle**.

It's impressive to see how the human body works and how the blood that flows from the heart flows into our lungs. When we ask Jesus to come into our hearts, our bodies become the temple of the Holy Spirit.

Just like the different chambers in our heart, the **outer court, inner court and the Holy of Holies** were separate chambers in the tabernacle of God. **Can you imagine how uncomfortable it is for The Holy Spirit when we cling to idols?**

How would *you* feel about sharing your home with a stranger? Just as you wouldn't let just anyone into your house, is the same way we shouldn't just allow anyone into our hearts.

It's okay for some people to stay in the living room when they come to visit you, and I'm sure only those closest to you would be allowed in your bedroom. The same could be said about those we allow into the most sacred place in our hearts, who see our vulnerabilities and to whom we tell our deepest secrets.

Give it time to heal

I love the effect time has on the human heart and brain. Over time you begin to forget who and what hurt you. As positive new memories form, love starts to heal you.

In my first book, *Beauty for Ashes*, I wrote that healing sometimes takes time. Although time is not the healer, I believe it can contribute to our healing. A physical wound eventually becomes a scar which serves as a memory of the pain experienced. But it no longer hurts.

Dealing with matters of the heart

The world tells you to follow your heart; the Bible tells us to guard the heart above all things. Who will you listen to?

When I reflect on the situation I almost got into with David, I ask myself why?

God had given me a prophetic word that I was going to get married through a stranger I met at an event, although she didn't say when. She also prophesied about other things that would occur next in my life. When she mentioned marriage, I ran over to a corner, in complete disbelief, and broke down in tears. It was something I had been praying about in secret, and all I had heard God say was to be patient.

'Don't cry.' She told me once she found me in the corner, I was hiding in.

'You don't understand... this is something that I've been praying about.' I said, sobbing but also trying to regain my composure.

'And of course, God heard you. Just like you have ears, so does He.' She said, smiling warmly.

I was so delighted. I kept thinking; *God likes to surprise me. He's heard my cry! I'm going to get married... I'm getting married.*

As I mentioned earlier that year had been full of disappointment in this area of my life, and I was losing hope. Her words filled me with hope for the joy I would experience on my wedding day.

These moments are so precious.

The problem was, shortly after this, I met David and well you know what happened there.

What the experience taught me was that when you entertain someone the enemy assigns, he starts using your fears to build strongholds, convincing you to compromise and settle for what the Lord has not sent. Having someone take an interest in me was comforting. It was like Brian (the last guy I dated) all over again, except things happened quicker and I fell faster and harder. But the spirit of God wouldn't let me rest, even though my weak flesh put up a fight.

In the end, David accused me of sending him mixed signals because I kept going back and forth, knowing deep within that God was saying 'I have closed the door.' Any relationship God hasn't ordained is unhealthy, so why go back?

The whole situation made me reflect on cycles in my life that needed breaking. I'll admit I was foolish, like that Ashanti song 'Foolish' where she sings about running back to a guy, she knew wasn't good for her. I was deceived into thinking that being sensible for so long hadn't gotten me anywhere. I also lacked intimacy with God at the time. Instead of focusing on rebuilding the intimacy and concentrating on my purpose, I was willing to give up everything for something I knew wouldn't last. How can something stand if it is built on a foundation other than Christ the Rock?

I was also scared about the future; not only with my relationships but life in general. I had a plan but, to be honest, I didn't know if it was going to work. I wanted assurance and security from somewhere, which was what David was promising me. It sounded like a win-win situation – he gets the girl of his dreams, and I get the ring, house, and marriage. All these were in my mind since he never actually offered any of these things, but that was where I was hoping things would end. I never had much stability growing up, so I'm attracted to men who I think can give me that.

God was so merciful and good to me during this time where I felt so lost and was searching for direction. Shortly after leaving my job, I got a new job. I remember telling God these exact words before sending my CV to the company.

"God, I want a job and I don't want to struggle for it."

Boy did He deliver, I was hired in less than two weeks after sending off my CV., which just goes to show what a good provider God is. My friend Nellia, had prayed with me on the morning of my interview and asked God for favour but I remember how upset I was after leaving the interview because I didn't think it went well, but God is faithful.

David was not a suitable match for me. When a situation doesn't work out the way we hoped it would, it's easy to believe the Enemy's lies that God doesn't love or is withholding something good from us. However, God's word tells us that every good gift comes from him. If a situation doesn't go the way we expected, it probably wasn't from God and wouldn't lead to our ultimate good. We must see God as a GOOD Father who wouldn't give us a snake if we ask for fish (Luke 11:11).

Your life is ultimately a result of the choices you make. It might hurt to hear this when we are so desperate that we are willing to get love at all costs with a reckless, risk-it-all mentality. Pray for patience. I've been doing that, and it's been helpful.

You must believe you are far too precious for God to give you to just anyone.

Black love - the narrative

What's wrong with the world, Mama?

People livin' like they ain't got no mamas

I think the whole world is addicted to the drama

Only attracted to the things that'll bring you trauma

Where is the Love, Black Eyed Peas

I get so happy to see black couples. It's beautiful when they look good together, but when they honour God's word together, it gives me hope.

Noughties' music videos and movies, on the other hand, sold dreams of young love without responsibility. No strings attached. There was no talk of real commitment, accountability or chastity.

Breakups, arguments, and make up sex are frequent media representations of black couples. They look great together, but there's no substance. The foundation is superficial and built on sand. No wonder it never works out.

The Bible tells us not to awaken love before its time (Song of Solomon 8:4), but how many times have I done this?

One of my cousins says a song 'Unappreciated' by an old girl group Cherish (ironic) reminds her of me; probably because I sang it repeatedly in secondary school. How sad is it that 14-year-old me could relate to feeling unappreciated in her relationship with a guy?

Some of us re-enact songs from such music videos when a guy mistreats us in adulthood. It feels so familiar because we may subconsciously believe we deserve to be taken for granted. That's why it's so essential for us to renew our minds.

Visible You

Young girl, young woman,

I know you're searching for significance, but you won't find it in him.

How could another human being, who is still figuring themselves out, show you who you are?

Young girl, I know you're searching for your purpose, but you can't find it in him.

Otherwise, you'll make him your lord, and he will tell you what you are good for.

He has no idea what your beginning was and what your end will be.

He has no clue.

All the thoughts that are woven together to make up your beautiful mind.

All the experiences that taught you how to be kind - even when others were cruel - that made up your sweet soul.

All the times, you felt like giving up, but you held onto hope.

As you held on, you realised that Love was holding on to you.

Who deceived you into thinking that you could find your life in a boy?

He noticed you because you were never invisible.

He was looking at what was on display.

A work of art. A masterpiece. A piece of the Master. A work in progress. You.

Can't you see that you existed before he came along?

Now that he's gone, why are you struggling to find **you**?

You. Yes, you. Visible you.

I know they told you Eve was taken from Adam, which led you to believe you are simply an extension of a man, and your purpose is to serve his needs.

But what if I told you that you have a higher call which you don't need a man to fulfil.

What if I told you that you are not merely an extension of a man but, instead, you are whole - all by yourself.

You weren't born incomplete.

You'll always have everything you need; and should you feel the need for companionship one day, that's all it'll be: companionship. Company.

Because You are whole

You. Yes, you.

(April 2020)

Not all men are trash, but they shouldn't be put on pedestals, either. Men are simply men. We don't have to put them down to feel superior. We are equally as powerful, intelligent and strong in Christ. Nor do we have to lift and hold them to a standard they cannot live up to. As women, we often see men as god-like figures capable of saving the world; and sometimes see ourselves as vulnerable damsels in distress.

The reality is you are not a damsel who needs saving. You are perfectly capable of handling whatever comes your way through Christ, who is your strength.

Colours

I used to love the song 'True Colours' by Cyndi Lauder.

What are **your** true colours?

Imagine your life from birth as a blank canvas to which you've been adding paint every day. We all want to paint a vibrant picture, full of life—celebrations, beauty, success and love—a little yellow, green, orange, and red. Isn't that what social media is portraying?

We desperately seek to add colour to the many shades of grey that paint our sometimes-mundane existence. But every day is not Friday and life is not always a party. At first, our bad decisions may make us feel alive; the drama we become involved in can be addictive. Instead of the brightness we want to experience, we paint the dirt and pain we're stuck in on canvases of muddy brown and black splotches.

So, we need to start over. It's a good thing the blood of Jesus can make our picture white as snow. If you're alive and with God, you can always reset and start painting again.

I shared this illustration with a friend of mine, and she reminded me that 'God is in the mundane'. Every new day can be an adventure with the Lord if we invite him into our day to day activities.

I think Romans 12:1-2 (TM) says it best:

'So, here's what I want you to do, God helping you: Take your everyday, ordinary

130

life—your sleeping, eating, going-to-work, and walking-around life—and place it before God as an offering. Embracing what God does for you is the best thing you can do for him. Don't become so well-adjusted to your culture that you fit into it without even thinking. Instead, fix your attention on God. You'll be changed from the inside out. Readily recognize what he wants from you, and quickly respond to it. Unlike the culture around you, always dragging you down to its level of immaturity, God brings the best out of you, develops well-formed maturity in you.'

True love heals

I'm not sure where you learned that love always hurts,

That love had to be dramatic, and that love was pain

I'm telling you love does not hurt at all

In fact, it heals.

Love makes you believe anything is possible

What you didn't understand,

What you failed to see, was that all those times you felt hurt was not me

I can use those situations to bring you closer, but I do not cause you harm

I cannot harm those I love

I am Love.

The very essence of my being and nature is not to harm you

But your previous experiences taught you to fear and not embrace me

I am the source of love

You run, you hide, you kick, you scream, you fight

But I'll still be here… still loving.

(August 2019)

On living your best life

What you do in secret matters the most. Who you are off social-media is far more important than who you appear to be on it, and being authentic is better than chasing after clout. **– Ebonys Proverb**

I like to attend events, go on adventures and go out to meals with friends. I am also profoundly moved by the sound of worship; I cry when I watch movies about love and get excited whenever someone mentions helping orphans. I believe your best life is lived when you have quality relationships. It is when you live with a sense of value and purpose, a deep reverence for God, and a grateful heart every day; having inner peace and joy independent of circumstances.

So, my question to you is one with which I challenge myself.

Are you living your best life?

Your best life begins on the inside, not externally. It is your spiritual life and relationship with God through Jesus.

Chapter 9: What to expect when you are a woman with a vision

'Where there is no vision, the people perish: but he that keepeth the law, happy is he' (Proverbs 29:18).

I once heard a man of God say vision is the reason, we get out of bed every morning. This idea that we are working towards something. I think some of the hardest questions to ask yourself are: Where am I heading in life? How can I achieve my goals? What is my purpose? We must write down our vision and make it plain.

Attacks from the enemy

Having a big vision can be very overwhelming at times. I went through a challenging season when I wanted to release my first book. Some people around me discouraged me from achieving my goal. It came as a massive shock because they were all leaders in my church. It broke me to the extent that I was no longer confident about who I was and where I was heading in life.

I made the mistake of believing the lie that their disapproval meant God had disapproved of my dream. At the time, I couldn't see God using the situation to redirect my path and surround me with people who would support me in more significant ways. If I'd given in to those negative voices, I would never have released my book and lives would not have been impacted.

The wilderness experience

I killed a slug today.

Without much thought, I poured salt on it.

I watched as it bubbled up and the salt melted its skin.

I buried it with so much salt; I thought it was over.

I carried on washing the dishes but then thought, 'let me just check to see if it's dead'.

I looked behind and noticed there was movement.

It was still alive. I could see the little antenna moving around.

What have I done?

Guilt.

The poor thing must have been in so much pain.

It's bizarre how it's so easy to kill a living creature and not care one bit.

Human callousness just shows how far we've fallen.

We never think God created that creature for a purpose.

It's not an accident.

It looks revolting, but it's actually a purposeful creature that is here for a reason.

Sometimes I feel like that slug.

Ugly.

People who are bigger than me think it's okay to pour salt on me and bury me.

But like the slug... I'm still alive.

They don't know it, though.

My guilt made me think twice.

I immediately thought 'maybe I can save it'.

So, to free it from the torment I had caused, I poured water on it,

Swept it into the dustpan and threw it out the window.

I did notice it was no longer moving around.

Perhaps it was dead.

Who knows whether the slug is dead or alive?

But I thought throwing it outside might provide a chance of survival.

Rather than leaving it there buried in the salt.

Isn't that what God does with us sometimes?

Sometimes you are like the slug.

Buried in your pain and sorrow.

He has to pick you up and throw you into the wild because he knows that, even though you're nearly dead, you have a better chance of surviving out there than under the salt.

(May 2018)

Looking back now, I was naïve. I recently read the book of Nehemiah in the Bible. God gave Nehemiah a burden to rebuild the walls in Israel and, after he fasted and prayed in repentance, God granted him all the resources needed for his mission. However, even though the Lord commissioned Nehemiah, enemies still attempted to oppose him. Nehemiah's response was to pray and re-strategize.

I believe someone reading this book has an assignment from God but is scared to step out because of something somebody else has said. I encourage you to discern whether that person is speaking from God or not.

Self-acceptance and self-belief are so important. There's no use going around begging others to notice or accept you. When you begin to shine, the right people will be drawn to you like a magnet. Not everyone will be your best friend but, that's okay, we are all on different journeys with different assignments.

Back in college, I befriended a girl in my law class called Naomi. She was kind, funny and caring. On one occasion, we began discussing our faith in class. She asked me to show her my hand. I did.

'Look at your fingerprint.' She said. 'Nobody in the world has the same fingerprint as you. You can't tell me there isn't a God.'

Everyone is uniquely created. It's okay if others do not understand your vision. God gave it to you, not them.

You may not be where you need to be because you are in the wrong environment

Just like a seed needs to be planted in an environment where it gets the right nutrients, direct sunlight and temperature to grow, so do you. Since environments mould and shape us, your environment must nurture, not stunt your growth. The people around you, especially your leaders, should bring out your potential. Do not allow people to box you into their limited view of who you are, based on short-sighted opinions.

According to the bible (Matthew 20:25-26 and 1 Peter 5:2-3), leaders should serve in humility and love, not try to lord it over you. They should identify your unique gifts and talents and respect your boundaries. You cannot allow people who didn't create you to define you. Do not be intimidated. Trust God be determined to grow and, if need be, move on.

Key things to remember

1. Do not be intimidated by the success of other women; your journey is unique and original.

2. Try your best to celebrate the achievements and successes of others. 'Rejoice with those who rejoice and weep with those who weep' (Romans 12:15).

A few years ago, I met a lady with a remarkable gift for celebrating other people's accomplishments. It was so infectious; I loved being around her. She made me feel good about myself and inspired me to be that kind of person to others. It's incredible what you will attract to yourself when you adopt this principle.

> 3. Whatever happens, let life make you better, not bitter. Bitterness stops you from moving forward.

Before releasing my book, I had to go through the process of forgiving the church leaders who put me down. I did this by praying for them. If you only view your life experiences from a subjective perspective, you will harbour things against people. There are spirits of wickedness that operate through people, unknown to them.

> 'For we do not wrestle against flesh and blood, but against principalities, against powers, against the rulers of the darkness of this age, against spiritual *hosts* of wickedness in the heavenly *places.*' (Ephesians 6:12 NKJV)

Distractions- *you must listen to the still small voice*

There were many challenges and so much confusion at certain points when I was going after my vision.

At such times, many voices speak to you at once, and it might be hard to distinguish God's voice from the enemy's lies. You must continue to fight! Remind yourself of who God is and what He told you to do.

A scene from the movie *Bird Box* ministered to me. (Spoiler alert) The movie is about an unseen force that makes people who look at it commit suicide. I know it's brutal, but there's a message here. The only way the characters survive is by covering their eyes – exactly how it is to walk by faith and not by sight. There's a scene where the protagonist, Sandra Bullock, and her two children are walking, blindfolded, in the middle of a forest, and the unseen force is coming after them. The little girl wanders off and hears the spirit (who sounds like her mother) telling her to remove her blindfold. It's intense because, at the same time, the mum is yelling at her to listen to *her* voice, and not the unseen force's. The scene was so powerful because you could hear the mother's desperation as she pleaded for her daughter to listen to her voice.

'Jesus says 'My sheep listen to my voice; I know them, and they follow me' (John 10:27 NLT).

I look back on when, I believe, God told me to leave the church I was attending. It was tough because I had my doubts, but once I made the decision, God confirmed I had made the right choice through people who had either received a word of knowledge or had a dream. Both were strangers.

There are so many loud voices out there, but we must listen to the Holy Spirit. His voice can be hard to discern when we are focusing on our present circumstances but, remember, God's voice is soft and gentle. God's voice is discerned not earned. He loves to speak to his children—we just need to recognise the way he speaks to us.

It's not so demanding, and He is not a taskmaster who wants slaves. He is a loving father who wants obedient sons and daughters.

Ask yourself: How long will you continue to live in fear? How long will you continue to be afraid of the opinions of others? The Bible teaches us that the fear of man is a snare - that means it's a trap. But trusting in God brings safety (Proverbs 29:25).

Despite opposition to writing my book from the people closest to me, I used to cry out to God: 'If I am your sheep, then I must know your voice'. But it was so hard to hear him with all the noise. When I told my friend Ren about this, she reminded me of what God had said over my life, and that 'giving birth was not easy.'

The power of focus

If you do not focus on specialising in a skill, you may become a Jack of All Trades, Master of None. Therefore, you must focus on doing one thing well. I am good at writing, but I am also good at baking. I discovered this when I started to bake while at university, and people complimented my cakes. Many people are gifted with multiple talents, but the reason they never reach their goals is that they cannot focus on one thing at a time. They are trying to do too many things all at once.

Just before I released my first book, I had a very confusing dream. I was on the underground, and I kept getting off and catching the train going in the opposite direction. I did this several times. I forgot about the dream until I was at an underground station with a friend when I suddenly remembered and told him about it.

'You're going in too many different directions.' He replied.

I was shocked that he accurately described my present state of mind. I hadn't thought about it that way before. At the time, I was dipping my hands into several projects at the same time and had begun questioning my next steps.

As if that wasn't enough, around that time, a lady at my church prayed for me. 'Focus.' She said as she hugged me tightly. 'If you focused, you would be where you want to be by now. Go home and concentrate on what God told you to do.'

I was hearing so many different voices speaking to me; it was confusing. That night, for example, I thought God wanted me to be in government. The only thing I *was* sure of: He had told me to 'tell the world my story'. I decided to persevere with that.

I always set goals for the new year, towards the end of every year. I try not to have too many because I know that, as driven as I am, external factors will come to distract me, and I will have to overcome obstacles.

Things to beware of when you set out towards your goals:

- Prepare to be tested
- Prepare to do it alone

- Remember God will send the right people

- Don't worry about finances

Lack of resources

People will not follow you because you have money. People will follow you because you have a vision. My friend Esther Adams has this saying: 'if it's God's will, it's God's bill.' I couldn't agree more. When I tell some people how I published my first book, they look at me in awe. They simply cannot comprehend the fact that people just gave me money. I was working part-time, earning less than £500 a month, when God told me to tell my story. I had a vision, and I knew that God would bring the provision. I just didn't know how. I'd written down the vision, calculated all the costs for the event, and knew exactly how I wanted my book launch to go.

I confided in a close friend and told her I was thinking of writing a book but didn't have enough money to finance it. She told me to send her a list of the resources I would need with a cost breakdown. I woke up the next morning to find a GoFundMe page circulating on Facebook set up by that very friend.

I called to thank her. She picked up almost straight away.

'Nyasha, I can't believe you. I woke up this morning to find that Ren had posted a link to a GoFundMe page, with my picture on it!'

'We cannot let a little thing like money get in the way of you writing this book, Ebz.' She said. 'Remember, it is a servant, not a master.' Our church had recently been teaching us this message.

I was so overwhelmed; I could feel my heart wanting to explode with joy.

'When you told me what you needed, I told the girls. I initially thought we could just split the cost, but they said it was too much. So, we each agreed to donate £50 when we get paid.'

'Thank you so much.' I was stunned by her kindness and thoughtfulness.

'It's the least I could do, Ebz.'

Within two months, I received over two thousand pounds from friends, family and strangers. It wasn't the first time God used complete strangers to bless me for his work. When I wanted to volunteer overseas in 2015, I appealed to my church, and a lady visiting the service gave me £100 towards my trip. Sometimes, I can hardly believe how incredibly blessed and favoured I am by God and people.

I think it's important to say that not all my friends gave me moral or financial support. I chose to overlook those because the enemy uses little things like that to cause arguments and make you question your worth. You are worthy—God wouldn't have come in the flesh to die for you if it wasn't true and He wouldn't have entrusted you with such a big vision if He didn't think you could achieve it.

God knew I needed that money, so He blessed me. He trusted me as a steward.

Money is a servant entrusted to you. I put the money I received for my first book in a separate bank account. However, because of the considerable delay in getting my book out, I dipped into it for other things, replacing it once I got paid from my day job. One day, I felt convicted about misusing the money. I sensed the Holy Spirit telling me that I was sad because I wasn't using the money for its intended purpose. That encouraged me to continue pushing to get my book finished.

Delay is not denial

There is nothing more powerful than a woman determined to rise.

'Hope deferred makes the heart sick, but a desire fulfilled is a tree of life' (Proverbs 13:12 NIV).

'God is within her; she will not fall. God will help her at the break of day' (Psalm 46:5 NIV).

'Consider it pure joy, my brothers and sisters, whenever you face trials of many kinds, because you know that the testing of your faith produces perseverance. Let perseverance finish its work so that you may be mature and complete, not lacking anything' (James 1:2 NIV).

Many people witnessed the release of my first book *Beauty for Ashes: An Exchange for Hope*, but what many do not know is the process I went through to publish it.

I began writing the book in November 2016 and wanted to publish it in August 2017, on my 24th birthday. However, things did not go to plan. A few months before I was supposed to publish my book, the editor returned my first manuscript and told me that she would advise me to rewrite the whole thing. This was humbling, as I knew I was a good writer, but I did need to develop my skill. Bear in mind there were only three months to the launch, I'd already put a deposit down for the venue and sent out my save-the-date invitations. Thankfully, I was able to get my deposit for the hall back as I had given enough notice.

At first, I couldn't see eye to eye with the editor, and all her probing questions made me so mad, but as time went on, I started to see that she had a point. The more I worked on the book, the better my writing became until finally, I produced something I could be proud of that others would enjoy reading. If I had rushed the process, I don't think the book would be as well-received as it is today.

God sent many people to encourage me and confirm his word to me during this period, for which I am grateful. One Sunday, I decided to attend the 11 am service at a church in Harlow. I had a cold and wasn't feeling too good, but I went anyway. I was slightly underwhelmed by the service, possibly because I was used to my church, but those who invited me were good people. After the service, I met my friend Samantha in the hallway. As we queued up for snacks, she introduced me to a few people.

'This is my friend,' Samantha said to a smiling lady behind us who was sporting a brown bobbed hairstyle. 'She's here for the first time.'

We shook hands. 'What's your name?' she asked.

'Ebony, what's yours?'

'Obehi.' She paused for a moment. 'Do you write?'

'Yes, I do.'

She nodded, then said, 'God says you should keep writing. It's going to help a lot of people.'

'Wow!' I wasn't expecting that. 'Did he say anything else?'

'No, he just told me "she writes".'

I was so encouraged.

People often compliment the front cover of *Beauty for Ashes*. And I admit that a great deal of thought and money went into it. But they don't know I faced many obstacles when I tried to upload it to the Kindle Direct publishing platform. There were issues with the picture's resolution quality and text alignment, as everything had to fit into a very tight margin for print.

With just three weeks to my book launch, I had to resubmit my cover five times in one week and, each time, wait up to twenty-four hours to ascertain whether it had been accepted. Every time my book was rejected, fear and anxiety tried to make me panic, but I had to push my feelings aside.

Thank God for my mentor who stood by me during this time. 'This book is going to be powerful.' She told me. 'Just look at the warfare.'

Breakthrough

During this challenging transition, I visited Pulse, my old church. One of the ministers prayed an uplifting prayer for discernment on who to work with during this time. One of my brothers in Christ also advised me to fast and pray as this was a spiritual battle. I obeyed this instruction and a friend of mine, joined me in fasting and prayer. I believe the principle in Matthew 18:19 was at work here.

I knew that I would have to persevere to receive my breakthrough. After several failed attempts at resubmitting my book cover, the paperback version of my book was finally approved on the 22nd of November 2018, the day after my sister's university graduation. I was distracted during the graduation dinner because my mentor and I were messaging each other as she helped me to upload it. I can't describe the joy and relief I felt the next day when I received the email that my book had been approved.

When giving birth to your vision, surround yourself with people who will help you push. I call them midwives. These people helped me believe that what looked like an impossible situation was possible.

I'm so grateful for the role they played during this difficult season.

The book launch

As the launch date approached, I realised things were a lot more expensive than I had initially budgeted for because of the venue change and food costs. When I confided in one of my mentors, she not only prayed for me, she unexpectedly deposited an additional £150 into my account.

I also found favour with the hotel managers. It was no coincidence that the lady dealing with me shared my surname. The staff were all accommodating. They even allowed me to customise my menu and didn't charge VAT for the food. God is faithful.

My book launch occurred at the Grange White Hall Hotel in Russell Square on December 8th, 2018, a year and three months later than I had planned. But I was ready by then and could face whatever came next as I'd completed the process.

When I asked a friend how she found the launch, she described it as, 'Very royal, like you.' I am so blessed to have loyal, supportive and creative family and friends who made it all possible. I borrowed chair covers from a friend for the day, and my friends Lynette and Ren helped me choose and order the decorations for my venue. One of my uncles picked up the balloons on that morning, and my friend Carl did the photography for free.

I still remember how happy I was as we drove to the venue that morning. Ren and I sang along to the latest Travis Greene song with Lynette quietly sitting in the backseat.

Smiling, Ren turned to me. 'God made the sun shine for you today.' Which was lovely, as it was winter.

We were met at the venue by my cousin Grace and her husband KC, who arrived early, to assist with the room set-up. It was all coming together so nicely.

Then the zip on the back of my dress split moments after a guest had shared a story of something similar happening to someone, she knew on their wedding day. What was strange about this was that the dress was purchased from a very high-end store's website.

We immediately rushed to the Ladies, where Grace and my friend Felicia tried to fix it. It was no use. It was stuck. Felicia, who was a fast thinker, suggested we go to a local dry cleaner.

'The devil is a liar.' Grace said as she waved me goodbye. 'Don't worry. Nothing will ruin this day for you.'

'Perhaps they can stitch up the dress with you wearing it.' Felicia suggested.

It was a ten-minute walk to the nearest dry cleaners, and we passed a few of my guests on the way, but I was exceptionally calm. I knew this was an opportunity for God to demonstrate his power and glory. At the first dry cleaning shop we found, the shopkeeper couldn't do the job at such short notice, so we went to another shop down the road. That one was closed.

'Okay,' Felicia said. 'Let's just go and find a new dress.'

We ended up at a New Look store where I immediately noticed a member of staff carrying a maroon jumpsuit.

I pointed it out to Felicia. 'What about that?'

We asked to see it. It was my size.

We looked at each other excitedly. 'Go, quickly try it on!' Felicia said.

I rushed to the changing room. To my surprise, the jumpsuit fit perfectly.

'Felicia! It fits!' I yelled, 'It fits!'

'Okay, take off the tag,' Felicia said. 'I'll pay for it at the till.'

To our surprise, the jumpsuit was on sale.

"You know, I'm agnostic, I'm not really sure if there's a God, but I might have to go to church on Sunday after that." Felicia said jokingly as we walked back to the hotel.

The launch began about thirty minutes late, but everything was smooth sailing from that point onwards. The host started with an icebreaker by asking the guests to discuss one thing they were grateful for. There were special guest ministers as well as a speaker. My mentor also gave words of encouragement. There was also a live Q&A where I took questions from the audience.

I am so grateful that I went through the preceding challenges. It made the victory so much sweeter!

Don't forget in the dark what God told you in the light

Just because something hasn't happened yet doesn't mean it will never happen, so try not to lose hope. You've got to remind yourself that delay is not denial. God is a generous Father who loves to bless his creation, there are many different reasons why we experience delays, but He always comes through, at the right time.

Joseph's testament (Genesis 37-50)

You may already be familiar with this story, but it's one that resonates with me. There was a boy, Joseph, who was destined for greatness. His father's favourite son, his father loved him so much that he bought him a beautiful multi-coloured robe.

God showed the young boy his future: he was going to be in a position of influence, and even his older brothers and father would bow down to him. However, Joseph made the mistake of telling his brothers his dream. Naturally, jealousy filled their hearts, and they plotted to kill him. At the last moment, one of his brothers showed him mercy and suggested throwing him into the pit instead.

The brothers then decided to sell him to Egyptian traders, and Joseph ended up in slavery to the Egyptians. While he was enslaved, he thrived and was given a high position. Unfortunately for Joseph, his master's wife was so attracted to him that she tried to sleep with him. Joseph refused her advances because he had respect for his master, which made her angry. As he ran from her, she tore off his robe, then told her husband Joseph had tried to rape her.

The master, Potiphar, threw Joseph into prison, where Joseph thrived and used his gift of interpreting dreams for others. One of his fellow inmates had a dream which Joseph interpreted, telling him he would be released from prison and restored to his position. The inmate was freed and reinstated; however, he promptly forgot all about Joseph. It wasn't until years later, when Pharaoh had a troubling dream that no one else could correctly interpret, that Joseph was summoned. God had revealed in Pharaoh's dream that there would be seven years of abundance, followed by seven years of great famine in the land. Because Joseph interpreted the dream, they were able to prepare and stock up for the future. Pharaoh honoured Joseph and made him the governor of Egypt.

Not only did Joseph save his family, but he also saved an entire nation. He understood that the evil his brothers intended against him had worked out for the good of many others. 'And we know that all things work together for good to them that love God, to them who are the called according to his purpose' (Romans 8:28).

Joseph's testimony is a prime example that the road to your destiny is not easy or straightforward, but it's worth it.

Joseph named one of his sons Manasseh, which means causing to forget for he said, 'God has made me forget my troubles and my father's house entirely.' He named his other son Ephraim which means fruitful, for he said 'God has made me fruitful in the land of my affliction.' Imagine being so blessed that you forget all your past trauma.

God took Joseph from the pit to the palace, from the palace to prison and from prison to become a governor of a nation.

The Bible doesn't explain how Joseph felt while these events were happening. It doesn't tell us of any moments of doubt about God's promise over his life. Anyone would understand if he did. All we see is that he remained faithful to God, which is evidence of Joseph's faith. This testimony inspires me so much, and it should inspire you, too!

Whatever hardship you may be facing right now is temporary. Your present situation does not determine your destination.

Another lesson the story teaches is that there is an appointed time for your breakthrough. Had Joseph been released from prison earlier, he might have missed his opportunity to speak to Pharaoh. You may be in a season where you feel discouraged or even be in a situation where those who were meant to help have forgotten you. The best advice I can give you is to pray and leave it to God. If he wants to use them to bless you, he will remind them at the right time. If he doesn't, He will use someone else! Through personal experiences and Joseph's witness, I'm learning that God's timing is always best, and so not to rush the process.

Another significant lesson we can learn from Joseph's story is that we must ignore the naysayers. Not everyone will be happy when you tell them your dreams, but their opinion is not enough to stop God's plan for you. Only you can do that through unbelief.

So, I'm asking you, 'who will you decide to believe?'

Let God be true, and every man a liar.

Chapter 10: Hey Queen

Heavy is the head that wears the crown - *Just because someone carries it well doesn't mean it isn't heavy.*

'If I perish, I perish.' - Queen Hadassah

You may be familiar with the story of Hadassah (commonly known as Esther) in the Bible. A young Jewish lady who goes undercover to the king's palace, Esther is known for her selfless bravery because she risked her life to save the Jewish people.

Esther's beauty led her to the king's palace, but courage made her a significant queen. In obedience to the call on her life, she persuaded the king not to annihilate the Jews, even though she could have been killed for flouting the law of the kingdom. She was unwilling to sit back and live in luxury while her people were in danger. This is the disposition of a woman of worth and virtue.

∞∞∞∞∞∞∞∞∞∞

'Hey, Queen.' Pareece said, smiling, as she greeted me one Monday evening at house fellowship. She said it casually, as though it was a matter of fact.

I loved Pareece's aura. She was always smiling, and you could tell her joy came from deep within.

I smiled back at her. 'I haven't even won the pageant yet!'

'That doesn't matter. You are still a queen." She said in that 'I'm-telling-you-this-until-you-believe-me' tone she used whenever she complimented me.

My friend Pareece Rose started calling me Queen before I even won the Miss E.B.O.N.Y. Ambassador pageant in July 2017. It always sounded strange to me.

I auditioned for the pageant in February that year, for several reasons.

1. I was bored and working part-time.

2. I wanted to participate in a project that would take me out of my comfort zone and develop my dancing and public speaking skills.

3. The winning prize – working on a skills development project in Nigeria – was enticing as I had never been to Nigeria.

4. I had just started writing my first book and thought it would be a great platform to promote it.

5. Pageants looked glamorous. My cousin participated in one in the past, and it looked like fun.

∞∞∞∞∞∞∞∞∞

In December 2016, I hit an all-time low after falling out with one of my uncles. We argued over something trivial, but I was convinced he hated me at the time. It was the first Christmas since my grandfather passed away and everyone was processing their grief differently. Emotions were high in our household.

My uncle had been lashing out at everyone, including my grandmother, which I didn't like.

'You shouldn't speak to Grandma like that.' I piped up.

'What? Who the f*** do you think you are?' He yelled.

I ran to my room, fearful that he might turn violent. On reflection, I realised it hadn't been the best time for me to speak up. I apologised to him by text, but he didn't respond. I knew he was still mad, so I kept my distance, even though we lived in the same household.
On Christmas day, I left his card in his room.

My grandmother called me over to the kitchen. 'Ope, take this food to your uncle.'

I did as I was told. My uncle was in the living room watching television. I placed the food on the table before him, and before I knew it, he started kicking off again.

'Who is this for?' He demanded.

'You.'

'How was I supposed to know it was for me?'

'I placed it in front of you.' I said.

He stood up. 'I don't know how you can call yourself a Christian when your heart is so dark. You want me to respect you? I have more respect for your younger sister. You'll never be a leader! From now on, don't say a word whenever you see me. And here's your stupid card!' He threw the card at me.

My mum, who was nearby, couldn't even defend me. She looked helpless.

I ran upstairs and hid in my room. My uncle had never been this spiteful and volatile towards me. Of course, we had our ups and downs, but he usually apologised. I respected and considered him an older brother since he wasn't that much older than me. His words cut deep.

What had I done to deserve this? I would be lying if I said suicidal thoughts didn't cross my mind. It was the lowest I had felt since recovering from my mental health breakdown. I confided in a few close friends and family members at the time. Their support encouraged and helped me temporarily. However, the pain followed me into 2017 like a dead weight.

One evening, I attended a worship night at a friend's church, but all I could do was sob in the presence of God. Then a young man approached me.

'I feel like you've had a hard time lately.' He said.

'Yes, I have.' I said softly, still weeping.

'Can I pray for you?'

I nodded so he closed his eyes and held my hands.

A few moments after he had said a prayer for me he opened his eyes and said 'You are going through this experience because you are going to help a lot of people. The devil does not want you to do this. He wants you to be self-conscious. God is saying you need to be God-conscious and look up.'

What my uncle said had caused me to question my very existence, but that prophetic word gave me the courage to go on. It was all making perfect sense now. **The devil attacks using the people closest to us because he knows it will hurt the most.**

∞∞∞∞∞∞∞∞∞

It was early afternoon on a weekday in 2017. I was studying my Bible in the living room when the doorbell rang. I was the only person downstairs, so I answered the door. It was *Iya* [5] Mary, one of my grandmother's friends.

I invited her in and gestured towards the living room. 'Grandma's upstairs. Let me tell her you're here.' I quickly ran up to my grandmother's room.

---

[5] Iya means mother in Yoruba so Iya Mary means the mother of Mary

'Tell her I will come down shortly.' Grandma instructed. 'Offer her a cup of tea.'

I went back downstairs. 'She'll be down soon.' I told Iya Mary. 'Would you like some tea?'

'No, thank you, dear.' She replied curtly.

I took a seat on the sofa opposite her and picked up my Bible.

'What are you reading?' She asked.

'The life of Joseph.'

She smiled at me. 'Opeyemi, I feel we should pray together.'

'Okay, Aunty.' I went to sit beside her. We held hands.

'Opeyemi, I see you rising above your peers.' She said. Her eyes were closed whilst she prayed.

'Amen! Thank you, Aunty.' I was very thankful for those words. I needed the encouragement as I was questioning whether or not to sign up for the pageant.

'You're welcome, dear. It's as though God wanted me to speak to you today. Tell Grandma I will come back later.' She rushed off.

Shortly afterwards, I entered the Miss E.B.O.N.Y. ambassador pageant and passed the audition stage. During our rehearsals and preparation for the pageant, Irene, the founder, often said things like: 'People think it is easy being a crowned queen. The moment we place this crown on your head, it means responsibility.'

I didn't fully digest the weight of her words at the time, but they foreshadowed the events to come. After months of preparation, it was finally the night of the finale. I don't think I or any of the other contestants felt ready. We all just wanted it over and done with. I could feel the nervous anticipation backstage as we did our hair and makeup and prepared our costumes. It had been a tough day, and we were running several hours behind schedule.

A lady wearing a purple and gold African-styled dress walked in the room. The atmosphere changed immediately. There was something regal about her. Her presence was so strong that you couldn't help engaging with every word she said. I later found out that she was the founder of a charity the pageant worked with.

'Let us pray.' She said in a strong South African accent. 'God, I thank you for every one of these young girls. Thank you for the day they were born...'

The day they were born... Those words triggered something in my soul.

When a new-born arrives, it is ordinarily a day of jubilation. However, as the child grows, the days that follow are often challenging, but nobody prepares the child for it. I thought back to all the events in my life that had led me to this very moment, and I was overwhelmed.

I had to step outside for a few moments to compose myself, but I could tell there was something special about this day, the 8th of July 2017. It was the day I was introduced to a new version of myself.

For the pageant, I pushed myself out of my comfort zone by making sure I did my research. To discuss my Nigerian heritage, I created a presentation. I was apprehensive when I first stood in front of the crowd but seeing my grandmother and my friend Bianca in the audience helped.

'My name is Ebony. I am from Nigeria in West Africa.' I pointed towards the map on the screen. 'My mum is originally from Osun State, and my dad is from Ekiti, the old Ondo state.'

The images on my PowerPoint presentation helped structure my points and made me feel more confident.

'Our traditional wear is called *Iro* and *Buba*, which is what I am wearing today.' I said, pointing at my outfit. I wore a royal blue wrapper around my waist, a white blouse and a blue and silver head wrap.

I went on to discuss our different cultural practices and the food we enjoyed eating. After I was done, some of the other contestants commented positively about my presentation and eloquence.

'I think that's what made you stand out.' Zara, a fellow contestant, told me after I had been announced the winner.

The previous queen, Aminata, whispered the words, 'Well done!' as she embraced me and placed the golden crown on my head. The rest of the night was a blur. Many people came to hug and congratulate me, but I couldn't tell you exactly what they said. I was in a state of disbelief and shock.

I spent the next two days locked in my room, crying before the Lord. They were healing tears. Something beautiful had blossomed out of all my pain and struggles, which was why I titled my first book *Beauty for Ashes*, from Isaiah 61 in the Bible.

Winning the pageant seemed to be a blessing and a curse. At first, the feeling was elating. My lifestyle changed overnight. I came home a crowned queen, and a week later, I was invited to the House of Commons to discuss youth violence. My participation was limited to listening at this meeting. Still, I used my influence to invite members of my church to a subsequent meeting on the same topic at the House of Commons. My church was passionate about rehabilitating ex-gang members and providing opportunities for young people. The discussions were with other members of the public, not MPs, so it was unclear whether what we had to say would make a difference.

'The kingdom of God is not a matter of talk but of power' (1 Corinthians 4:20 NIV). Unless you see a real change, you begin to feel like you're just a figurehead with no real power.

Goals-wise, I would say my public speaking skills improved, but not my self-confidence. I went from feeling insignificant to having people stare at my crown whenever I entered the room. It was overwhelming at times, and I struggled to know who I was when I took it off. It almost became a mask. I struggled with what it meant to be a queen and who I was without the crown. Whenever I took it off, I felt irrelevant. It was lonely.

It's safe to say the crown was becoming an idol. I tried my best to keep it together, but I realised I wasn't secure in my identity in Christ when, six months into my title, on the train returning from visiting a friend in Leicester, I broke down in tears.

The great Nelson Mandela once said, 'Overcoming poverty is not a gesture of charity. It is an act of justice.

It is the protection of a fundamental human right, the right to dignity and a decent life6.'

Despite being overwhelmed, I pushed through and managed to raise money towards my mission trip to Nigeria. Although the pageant was responsible for the majority of the fundraising via their 'Go Fund Me' page, I also played my part by holding a cupcake sale at my place of work.

I travelled to Nigeria on the 3rd of March 2018. Early that morning, Benjamin, the cousin of Irene (the pageant's founder), picked me up and escorted me to the airport. I was going for 19 days, so I packed as many clothes as possible into one large suitcase and one piece of hand luggage, only for Irene to inform me that I could only use my hand luggage. We needed a big suitcase for the children's clothes, which I must have forgotten. This meant the nearly impossible task of squeezing as many clothes as possible from my big suitcase into the hand luggage case at the airport and then making sure the suitcase wasn't overloaded. I took some pictures with Irene, and she waved me off.

As I passed through customs, I noticed that my hand luggage was held up. I started to panic. My flight was at 8.40am, and time was ticking. As the lady unpacked my case, I realised that, in all the flurry, I forgot that liquids were not allowed in hand luggage.

6

http://www.mandela.gov.za/mandela_speeches/2005/050203_poverty.htm

There went my bio-oil and body cream. When she was done, I looked up at the nearby analogue clock. It was 8.15am. I wasn't sure if I was going to make the flight.

I hurriedly tried to squeeze my belongings back into the suitcase, but I couldn't close it properly. Panicking, I tried to find the gate. Just then, an announcement came on the tannoy system.

'Last call for Ebony Ali to gate 58.' The lady said.

Clothes hanging out of my suitcase, I ran to the gate as though my life depended on it. I was the last person to board the plane, this was only by the grace of God.

After we landed at the airport in Lagos, a man approached me while I was collecting my suitcase.

'Do you need help?'

'Yes, please.' I replied.

He picked out my suitcases and placed them on the trolley. 'Where are you from? America?'

'England.' I replied. Something felt off, but I couldn't quite put my finger on it.

He walked me to the customs area and stopped. 'That will be 20 dollars.'

'20 dollars? For what?' I was astounded.

'That is what it costs for me to help you with your luggage.' He said matter-of-factly.

'I only have pounds, not dollars, I'm afraid.' I replied.

'That's fine, it's the same thing.' He said.

I was being robbed, but I honestly did not know what to do.

'I need to go to the toilet first.' I told him.

'Okay, I will wait here with your stuff.' He said.

I found the nearest toilet, took out my phone and tried connecting to the WIFI to contact my dad, who was picking me up from the airport. There was no reception. So when I walked out, I reluctantly handed the stranger a £20 note.

'It is because of love that I only charged you £20. So, where is my fee? It's another £20.' I could not believe the man's audacity.

'You're mad.' I grabbed the trolly, kissed my teeth and headed towards customs.

An officer there stopped me. 'Open the suitcase for me.' I reluctantly complied.

'What are all these clothes for?' the officer inquired.

'They are for charity, Sah.' I responded in the best Nigerian accent I could muster.

'What about me? Where is my own?' I handed him a £20 note.

'Okay, you can go.' He said.

This was beginning to feel like a nightmare; my very first-time visiting Nigeria, and I was duped twice within 20 minutes. I had heard about the corruption in the country but now was experiencing it first-hand.

When my dad arrived, I told him everything. He was livid.

'Someone should have warned you about this! It's that sombrero you're wearing.' Dad added. 'They know you are not from here.'

'I only wore it because it wouldn't fit in my suitcase.'

Dad reported what happened to a security guard, but there was not much he could do. I watched noticing how my dad skilfully tipped the guard for doing his job. The guy who had 'helped' me with my luggage had vanished and, well, the customs officers were just as corrupt.

'Twenty pounds! Do you know how much that is worth in Nigeria?' Dad said as we drove away from the airport. He was still fuming. 'The guy has probably never seen that much money in his life!'

I'm sure you can imagine just how angry I was. At the same time, I couldn't help thinking how desperate these people were to defraud their own people.

As we drove to my uncle's house where we would be staying, I gazed out the window, taking in the rural landscape. Nigeria is very dusty.

When we arrived at the house, Dad introduced me to Taiwo, a fair-complexioned lady with beautiful green eyes and Yetunde, her dark skinned and slender friend. I'm always amazed by how diverse Nigerians look.

'I have hired them to look after you.' Dad proudly proclaimed. 'Nigeria is not a safe place like London.'

Taiwo was my uncle's sister in law. They were true destiny helpers who cooked my meals whenever we were at the house. They helped me fix my crown before meetings, carried our luggage to the charities, and showed me around Lagos on my days off.

One night, they stayed with me in a hotel near the first school we visited.

'Hide your money in your Bible.' Taiwo suggested
.

I felt like I was in one of those movies, where the main characters are on the run from criminals. As if someone would bust open our door in the middle of the night demanding we give them all our money.

We were always laughing together. I am very grateful for the two ladies. Travelling around was quite stressful. There were days when I had to be up in the morning while it was still dark and skip breakfast because I had three appointments in one day. I usually enjoy hot weather, but I wasn't used to the Nigerian climate, which put a massive strain on me. The traffic was also ridiculous – we were often held up for hours at a time.

The attention I received at different events with people continuously wanting to take pictures with me or interview me was draining. Having Taiwo and Yetunde's support helped immensely, as they could see my humanity. I was amazed by how much two people who hardly knew me demonstrated such genuine love. I believe God will reward them for this.

I was also fortunate to have a lady from London whom I called 'Aunty Victoria' join me on the trip. She was closely affiliated with the pageant and helped me manage my wellbeing. She showed me around Lekki, the posh part of Lagos, where she had relatives with whom we stayed.

It's shocking to see the difference between Lekki and Ikorodu where my dad's brother was situated – Lekki was like Beverly Hills, and Ikorodu was like the ghetto. It's one thing watching it on a documentary, it's another seeing it with your own eyes. Ikorodu did have its perks, though, catching lifts on the back of motorbikes was one of them.

'You need to learn how to manage crises.' She would tell me when she noticed how stressed I was. She was right, but I also needed to rest.

Visiting the orphanage and primary schools in Nigeria was one of the most rewarding experiences I've had in my life. I was able to encourage the children, who were so ambitious, bright and full of life, to work towards fulfilling their dreams and helping one another. The children at the orphanage shared their dreams with me. One wanted to be a fashion designer another a teacher.

Two songs became a refrain during my stay in Nigeria. One was Michael Jackson's *Man in the Mirror*, and the other *Teach Me How to Pray* by Jason Upton. Both songs emphasise our responsibility for the state of the world and the need to make a change through self-reflection, acts of charity, and, in Jason's case, intercessory prayer.

On my way back to the UK, I misplaced my crown, which I had been carrying in a hand luggage case, at the airport in Amsterdam. I searched around the seating area, but it was nowhere to be found. However, instead of feeling sad, I felt as though a huge burden had been lifted off me.

I arrived in the UK just before 8 am. While collecting my suitcase from the luggage area, I glanced at my phone. The verse of the day on my bible app was 'Blessed is the man who perseveres under trial, because when he has stood the test, he will receive the crown of life that God has promised to those who love him' James 1:12 (NIV).

You are not a queen because of your title or crown, you are a queen because of who you are inside.

How Ironic, I thought. I had just lost my physical crown, and here God was talking about giving me an eternal crown for persevering through the trials of life.

At that moment, I decided I had completed my pageant commitments and no longer wanted to attend interviews and events. Irene and I then agreed that my only outstanding responsibility would be to hand over my crown to the new queen at the finale.

Being so busy with church and pageant commitments put a considerable strain on me. I was also frustrated because releasing my first book was taking a lot longer than anticipated, and the thought of it not happening was extremely worrying. Making a comeback after a severe mental health episode like mine wasn't easy. Instead of simply embracing the process, I put myself under immense pressure, believing I had something to prove to myself and others.

I wanted to give up, but every time I tried, something (I believe it was the Holy Spirit) rose in me, and I had to continue.

One morning, I woke up and began to understand what God was saying through the events in my life. *'You are not a queen because of your title or crown; you are a queen because of who you are inside.'*

This was a huge wake-up call.

Growing up the way I did left me broken. I looked for validation and approval in my friendships with other women because, as a child, I received little praise and validation from my mother (this is no longer the case today). Imagine realising this about yourself at twenty-four. It was a huge shock. Any kind of separation from close female friends triggered anxiety, and my deep-rooted abandonment issues flared up.

The pain was intense.

'God, don't leave me,' I cried out on my bed one evening in June. It was the night the new Miss E.B.O.N.Y. Ambassador was to be crowned. I had a mini breakdown while getting ready.

'I can't.' The Holy Spirit replied.

Okay. I put on my brave face and went to the event.

Knowing God was with me gave me the strength to go on, but my emotions were not lining up, and it wasn't long before I was triggered again. It seemed to be a never-ending cycle, so much so that the friend who triggered me would say, 'this will never stop!' My friend no longer believed I could change, but God didn't give up on me.

A friend eventually referred me to a counsellor from her church, so I reached out to her. My story so moved her that she decided to counsel me for free. We began weekly counselling sessions, where I opened up about my childhood, my relationship with my parents and God. We discussed my brokenness in friendship and my hopes and dreams for the future. She encouraged me to spend time with God and helped to put a lot of things in perspective.

'You realise Nancy is not your mum.'

Nancy, one of my best friends, and I had been drifting apart, and it hurt so much. I felt she had abandoned me for the church and her new friends, and I had nothing left. I had blocked her number on several occasions and had even changed my number and not given it to her. I can see how spiteful that was now, but I've realised that blocking someone doesn't block the pain, it just buries it.

This led to several bitter, passive-aggressive arguments between us throughout the year, and I could tell she was fed up. The friendship became toxic and was no longer healthy for either of us.

I had to learn to separate my identity from my present actions and my friend's perception of me. I also had to forgive myself for the hurtful ways I treated her. It was the only way I could move forward.

When I listened to a podcast by a famous influencer discussing how, after he realised love was a choice, he confronted his gang rivals armed only with the words, 'I love you, and we've been lied to'. He left the gang that day, unharmed.

I realised love is not based on feelings but a decision to act lovingly towards others, regardless of the way they treat us. I continued to pray that I could forgive my friend, and I eventually did, but I still had to let her go.

The power of love

I freed myself to pursue my purpose passionately without my friend's cheerleading.

I realised I had reached a level of healing when I could move on with my life without her validation. I no longer reacted from a place of pain and bitterness. Sometimes, it's best to give ourselves closure by no longer dwelling on things we cannot change and moving forward.

Even youths grow tired and weary, and young men stumble and fall; but those who hope in the LORD will renew their strength. They will soar on wings like eagles; they will run and not grow weary; they will walk and not be faint. Isaiah 40:30-31

Flying Lessons

I guess you could say I was down on my luck when we first met. An angel who had forgotten how to fly. My rusty and fragile wings curved around me in case they still had to protect me from the fiery darts that had damaged me during the last battle. Boy, did they hurt!

But then, I met you. Your eyes shone bright as you asked me a question.

I responded, all defences down, allowing you to see into the deep darkness of my soul.

The flicker of light in your eyes as you told me your story assured me that there was hope for me to fly again.

I saw your pain, but you loved me as you had never suffered loss. It was as though your heart had never been broken. That healed me, I tell you, it did. It reminded me of friendship and companionship, the ability to trust, and that I am never alone. To trust in a divine connection and believe it's still worth it after all we've both been through.

Love. That four-letter word that means everything to us. The reason we breathe. The reason we live. The only thing worth giving our lives for.

Love. I needed to believe in something bigger than me. I needed the courage... to fly again.

Thank you. For teaching me how to fly. Thank you for showing me the way.

Thank you.

Like a phoenix from the ashes, I began to rise. I was so surprised to see my feet lift off from the ground. And you were there, right beside me, my companion, cheering me on from the side-lines. I'd been on the ground far too long; I'd forgotten how good it felt to fly, high. Forgotten how the gentle breeze felt on my face and how weightless I felt up there in the sky.

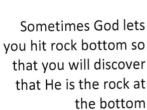

Sometimes God lets you hit rock bottom so that you will discover that He is the rock at the bottom

\- Tony Evans

Freedom.

I looked around; we were in an open space. Others were also learning how to fly.

I turned left, but you went right towards them. I watched you give them a hand. It was time for you to teach them how to fly.

I panicked, and my heart began to sink. Before I knew it, I was falling, fast.

'Come back! Save me! I'm falling.'

But you were too far away to hear my desperate pleas for help.

I fell faster. 'I don't think I can make it on my own!' I squealed. Suddenly, I hit something that felt like rock bottom but, to my surprise, I was unharmed.

I sat down and took camp on the sturdy rock. It wasn't comfortable, but it gave me time to figure out what just happened.

Days and nights went by. Many troublesome thoughts filled my mind. If I could just get back up there, maybe we could fly together again. But I had no idea where you were, or in what direction you were heading, which scared me. As I sat there contemplating how on earth, I ended up down here again, it hit me that it was impossible to focus on flying and on you at the same time.

I knew what I had to do. I had to let you go. The decision freed my mind, and my wings began to flutter. The more I thought about flying, the more they moved until they shot right up. I had to rely on whoever gave me my wings in the first place, and trust that I would reach my destination safely.

I call him God. Somehow, I lost sight of the bigger picture and assumed he left when you did.

As I stood up from the rock and gazed at the clear blue sky, a voice as soothing as the gentle tide whispered, 'Are you ready for your flying lesson?'

'Yes Lord, I am.' I replied.

Real Confidence

I gathered with my family and friends for a meal one Bank Holiday Monday in 2018. We were sitting around the table when my younger cousin, who was five or six at the time, randomly started chanting, 'I am confident, I am real'. It was so infectious that we all joined in.

It's remarkable how God speaks to us in these moments. I had just returned from my mission trip to

Nigeria. While over there, I fell out with Nancy because she said she would call me the morning of my trip, but she hadn't. I was upset about this but didn't know how to confront her about it, so when I asked her how she was doing after she told me she hadn't been feeling well, she said I wasn't genuine. Although, I was genuinely concerned about her health, I was also hurt but what she said had affected my confidence. There I went, doubting myself again.

It was a timely word. 'You know when the Holy Spirit has to teach you this at an early age...' I said to my older cousin.

I wonder what kind of woman I would now be if I had learned to affirm myself earlier on in life. But it's not too late. I can still become who I'm meant to be, and so can you!

No matter how you feel, get up, dress up and show up. Our confidence tends to increase when we are dressed up. As my cousin used to say, 'If you look good, you feel good.' However, it must go beyond this. Irrespective of our appearance, we must remain confident. Real confidence is an inside job, and true confidence comes from putting your trust in God.

You cannot depend on your feelings when it comes to becoming a committed and consistent person.

Confidence is not a cloak you put on to mask how you feel inside. Real confidence is a state of being that comes from a way of thinking about who you are and the world around you. You must be at peace with yourself.

Affirmation for confidence: **I am a product of a Creative Mastermind; therefore, I can do all that He has asked of me. I can do and be anything with God!**

Wise stewardship

Your life is God's gift to you, but what you do with it is your gift to God.

God is expecting a return on his investment in you. Our time on earth is short, but it doesn't have to be meaningless. Time is our most precious commodity; we will have to account for how we've spent it.

So, learn to be a good steward of time.

Years ago, when I had drifted away from God, I had a dream in which someone who represented God was asking my former church Youth Leader, Ian, what he did in his spare time. Ian replied that he had brought these

Don't fake it till you make it - BECOME.

'little ones' (which included me) to him.

I remember thinking in the dream, 'Oh, please don't ask me what I do in my spare time!' because I was so ashamed. I woke up with my mind completely renewed, the words *Now I know what it means to fear God and not people* - firmly imprinted on it.

That wasn't how I wanted to meet my maker, full of fear, shame and regret. I wanted to die empty, having poured out everything God placed in me from before I was in my mother's womb. I needed to change.

I eventually did – one decision at a time.

Maximise your time

'Make the most out of every opportunity, redeeming the time because the days are evil' (Ephesians 5:16).

You may think you have all the time in the world, but you don't. We pray for long life and good health, but no one knows when their time is up, and it's time to leave this earth. Many young people waste time on foolish things. Instead of building towards their future, they indulge in activities that do not add value to them. They spend time partying and getting drunk, and think to themselves, 'At least I enjoyed my youth'.

I believe in enjoying yourself but drinking alcohol excessively and sleeping around is not wise. It never ends well. I've seen people younger than me achieving great things for the kingdom of God. Do you want to know what their secret is?

Not only did they have the foresight to attain wisdom early on, but they also chose to

Your life is God's gift to you, but what you do with it is your gift to God.

become disciples under the right spiritual leaders and mentors. They knew there would be sacrifices to make if they wanted to achieve great things early in life. They would need to say, 'I cannot do what others my age are doing'. Without sacrifice, we remain stagnant and ineffective. I commend them for having the positive attitude that brings growth and purpose.

We have 24 hours in a day, enough time to do the things we want or need to do. Instead, of playing games on your phone or scrolling through social media, why not cut that time in half and use your lunch breaks to work towards a goal? You'll feel better for it!

I don't get much signal on my phone when I'm travelling underground, so if I have a book, I use that time to read. It's become a habit.

Life can be a ferocious bull that needs taming. Do you want to know how to take the bull by its horns? The best way to drive your life in the right direction is to submit everything to God. You can't lose with him on your side.

Knowing where and who to invest your time in is crucial if you want to get ahead in life.

Lessons from The Lion King

Lions are brave; they dominate the jungle.

What I learned from watching The Lion King in 2019 is that Simba knew he was called to reign but shied away from his responsibility because of two things: fear and shame.

In the film we see Simba (a lion) eating the same foods consumed by Timon the meerkat and Pumba, a warthog, after he had run away from home. One day, Simba sees his father Mufasa, the bravest lion that ever lived, in his own reflection in the river. Mufasa speaks to him from beyond the grave and tells him to: 'Remember who you are'. From this, Simba finds the courage to go back home and face the person he is most afraid of. A whole tribe was depending on his return and similarly to Simba, there is a generation dependant on your obedience to the call of God on your life.

Do you know what our God is called? THE LION OF THE TRIBE OF JUDAH!

Do you know who **you** are, Daughter of God?

When the truth settles deep within your heart, it causes strength and courage to arise; and fear and shame must bow down. There comes a time where every person must rise to fulfil their destiny. We cannot run away from what and who God has called us to be. There is too much at stake.

Ebony's Top Tips

1. Learn to rise above feelings and perceptions. They are not always true. You are likely to develop certain sensitivities and viewpoints based on whatever trauma you have experienced.

2. Forget fantasy. Focus on what is real and tangible, what is happening right now, and what you can do with what you've been given.

3. Practice gratitude.

4. Allow God to meet your needs.

Chapter 11: Rediscovering yourself

It takes courage to grow up and become who you are.

-EE
Cummings

To find out who you are, you must first find out who you are not – Toure Roberts

I'm continually learning new things about myself; especially my likes and dislikes.

Stripping away what is not you helps you discover what is. Throughout much of life, we pick up traits from other people; adopting their values and thoughts as our own. We settle for being carbon copies of others rather than being original versions of ourselves. I believe we must learn to embrace our own personalities. If you're co-dependent, you may find this difficult, but freedom is found in being your authentic self.

In rediscovering myself, I realised that I am quite girly. I like the colour pink, dressing feminine, and things that glitter and sparkle. As a teenager, my email address was *glitterteen,* but I later tagged myself as *ladyshady* and *ladyting* as I started to follow the trends of my friends. I hid this part of me for a long time because I wanted approval from my peers. A friend told me she liked wearing dark-coloured clothes, so I decided I liked dark colours, too. Another friend thought dark hair would suit my dark skin and enhance my complexion, so I stuck to black hair for a while. But none of these were me. I allowed other people's opinions to shape how I physically adorned myself.

Although, I do like wearing dark colours, I also like bright colours and, sometimes, bright hair. My first mobile phone was pink. I prefer wearing heeled boots to trainers. I don't wear makeup every day, but I appreciate the art form.

If this is true about changing our outward appearance, how many people change core values to suit the opinions of those around them? This is dangerous.

My mother says loyalty is one of my core values. 'It seems to affect you when people are disloyal to you. It hurts you deeply.' She would say whenever I opened up to her about mishaps with friends.

Do you know your core values? Understanding them helps you choose relationships more effectively. We are all unique. I want you to celebrate this instead of hiding parts of yourself because you need the approval of others.

Words of affirmation: our declarations of faith

'Death and life are in the power of the tongue: and they that love it shall eat the fruit thereof' (Proverbs 18:21).

In 2019, when I began to write down and speak my desires out loud, I saw a massive shift in my life. I experienced radical growth and the manifestation of those desires in line with God's will.

I believe that speaking them out loud caused my heart to believe what I said. I also noticed things around me shifting, and what once seemed impossible suddenly seemed possible. I now understand why people say to 'be careful what you ask for'.

Speaking to a friend over WhatsApp about our celebrity influences and journeys with God, I told her that I commented on a famous actress' Instagram post and the actress had replied. My friend's response was along the lines of 'you will meet her'.

'Amen!' I replied.

I didn't think much of it but, later that year, I received a message on Instagram inviting me to a film premiere the actress was attending in London. I attended the event, spoke to the actress, and gave her a copy of my book. Amazing things happen when you speak words of faith.

That actress, who is also a Christian, said something to the audience that day that stayed with me. 'We deserve God's best because

I am a product of a Creative Mastermind, therefore, I can do all that He has asked of me. I can do and be anything with God

—Ebony Ali

He says we do.' She also said, 'Do not wait till you have the resources to start working towards your vision. If not now, when?' which was the name of the movie she had produced and starred in.

Say NO to excuses - rise to challenges that present themselves

That same year, I delivered my first book writing workshop to a group of teenagers at a summer school for Sapphire Community Group. It was the first time I delivered anything like this. I was so excited.

I had to produce the presentation with short notice, and I almost missed out on the opportunity because I did not like being out of my comfort zone. But an inner voice (I believe it was God) told me to go. After the workshop, I decided to push myself to the next level and start marketing myself as a workshop facilitator—something I had never even thought of doing before.

Be a blessing to others

Don't be selfish. Share what you have with other people, and more will be given to you. Do not neglect this principle of life! It may not come naturally, but practice makes perfect. The more you practice it, the easier the principle becomes.

You have a wealth of knowledge, experience and expertise that others are just dying to access; but some won't ask because of pride, fear and misconceptions. However, when someone does ask, be that generous woman. The Bible tells us 'A generous person will prosper; whoever refreshes others will be refreshed'

(Proverbs 11:25 NIV). You receive a blessing when you help others.

In 2020, a lady reached out to me on Instagram as she was in the process of writing a book. I genuinely enjoy helping others succeed, so I gave her some tips and advice. A few months later she let me know that she was releasing a jewellery line and she wanted to give me some jewellery as a gift because I had been kind to her. I thought it was sweet. However, it doesn't stop there, a few months later, she reached out to me again and offered me a nights stay in a 5* luxury hotel for free. I could hardly believe it! She had initially booked the hotel with some of her family members; however, they were no longer able to attend, and she thought of me. This was in the middle of a global pandemic, so the time away was much appreciated as travelling abroad was limited and I love travelling. You just don't know how God is going to bless you, if that isn't the favour of God, then I don't know what is!

I also believe that when you give sacrificially, there is a reward. I remember a stage in my life when there was a call at my church fellowship to give a 'costly seed.' I had recently learned about the power of giving in faith. I had just finished working very long shifts as a steward in the O2, but I felt led to give my entire earnings in the offering. Then I went home and cried. As I wept, the Holy Spirit reminded me of my connection with an organisation that supports young people and prompted me to contact them.

When I visited their headquarters, the man leading the project offered me a £350 bursary towards anything I needed to achieve my goals.

I told him I needed an iPad to write my book.

'Yes, we can do that.'

A few days later, I received an iPad that was worth almost double the amount I had given. I was so amazed by what God had done through my simple act of obedience.

Use your initiative

Do you want to know one reason you may not be where you want to be? Maybe you are not using your initiative.

Lazy people cannot prosper.

'A little sleep, a little slumber, a little folding of the hands to rest so shall your poverty come like a prowler, and your need like an armed man' (Proverbs 24:33-34).

Laziness is defined as

- being unwilling to work or use energy, characterised by lack of effort or activity.
- Showing lack of care, disinclined to work or exertion (physical or mental effort).
- Encouraging inactivity or indolence.

So, what is the opposite of laziness: hard work and self-discipline? If I were to introduce someone to an opportunity, I would like them to show some initiative and not expect me to do the work for them. I want to help you succeed, but I cannot want to help you more than you want to help yourself. I will do what I can, but we each have a course to run, and I cannot afford to let others drain me.

Fan into flame the gift of God inside you and do not despise the days of humble beginnings.

After years of not feeling 'good enough', I started my blog in 2016. I did not have many readers, but I did it for the love of writing. Looking back, I was developing my gift and preparing to write a book.

Being a woman of your word

Do what you said you would, long after the mood you said it in has passed.

I cannot stand it when people close to me do not keep their promises. I'm learning to cut people some slack because I, too, struggle with this. However, it's not a trait I admire in myself or others. It ruins trust and breaks down relationships.

I know people sometimes hold us to a standard we cannot attain. Still, *you* set the tone of any relationship and teach people how to treat you, so teach them to treat you well by treating them well. Teach people to value your time and effort. Keep close only quality people who understand these principles and are willing to pay the price.

I understand that human beings can have an unfortunate trait of over-committing, but we must do better!

I know I'm passionate about this but, just imagine. If we all tried to keep our words, there would be fewer disappointments, and we would uphold our integrity.

Love is a verb

You deserve the best kind of love.

Love is proved sincere through actions, so don't just tell me you love me. Show me. Some people say they love you, but through their actions, you know they do not, at least not in the way that you need to be loved.

This leads to disappointment and, sometimes, bitterness.

If someone keeps cancelling an arrangement we've made, I will start to feel they do not value my time, or they are unorganised. Neither trait is attractive to me. However, I recognise that circumstances which are out of their control can affect the person's decision-making, so it's always best to be gracious.

Mistakes happen, and there's grace, but I tend not to be too close with people who know something hurts me but refuse to change or rethink their actions. Nor should you be! I do, however, love to embrace those who have a sincere change of heart. I will repeatedly forgive you without letting you walk all over me and infringe on my boundaries.

If that makes me hard to love, then that's perfectly fine. It might mean your season in my life has ended. Kindly exit the building and close the door when you leave. I expect so much because I give and love so much. I know what I bring to the table.

Does this sound familiar? Isn't this how God treats us?

It all goes back to value. Ladies let's raise the standard of love.

The importance of professionalism

It is imperative to remain professional if you are a businesswoman. You cannot successfully do business if you are insecure and need others to affirm you.

Everything is a choice. You can either let others inspire or depress you. Everyone loves consistency and reliability, so don't be flaky. If you make appointments with clients, try your best to keep them! People will respect you more if you show up on difficult as well as good days. Of course, there are situations when we may need to cancel, just don't make it a habit.

Send your invoices on time - do not delay - efficiency is everything! Do not make your clients chase you down; they may lose respect for your business. Try to respond to emails within 24 hours, dedicate time for this.

Don't keep your customers waiting; be on time. Remember you are representing your company or brand, and you need to embody it well!

Dress the part—how you show up in the world is crucial. God looks at the heart, but people judge us by our outward appearance. In business, how you present yourself is pivotal to how others will receive you. It will also affect how confident you come across.

Faith without works is dead. You must make God your driving force *and* take intentional steps towards your destiny.

Sometimes you have to get quiet when building anything of value. Share your successes with a few trusted people but, most times, make silent moves. Remember, you are living for the audience of One. What you do in secret, your father will reward openly.

Your creativity is your currency

'**Opportunity comes to those who create it.**' Charlamagne Tha God, author of *Black Privilege*.

There will be times in your life when opportunities will come to you, and times when you have to create them. I believe both are from God. That doesn't mean that you should do things without consulting him. We must remember to acknowledge him and trust that he'll guide us along the right path.

Many of the opportunities I've had to promote my book have come to me. From radio interviews, holding book signing events at WHSMITH stores across London to being interviewed on the DMD talkshow on BenTV. I didn't go looking for them, but God opened those doors of opportunity for me. The most effort I made was when I was featured in my local Newspaper *The Hackney Gazette* in June 2019. This was after a friend suggested I write up a press release and send it to news outlets (Those Journalism skills came handy.)

> Opportunity comes to those who create it.
>
> Charlamagne Tha God

Your gift *will* make room for you, but you may need to showcase it. Social media can be a useful tool for this. It's also helpful to connect with different people by networking and supporting other people's events. Use what you have to create the life you want.

Organisation

I've had a diary almost every year since I was sixteen years old. I sometimes think I'm too reliant on it, but I would find it difficult to keep on top of my plans if I didn't write them down.

Use a diary to plan your days, weeks and months. Being disorganised is expensive – it can cost you opportunities.

How to handle your interpersonal relationships

Try not to assume someone dislikes you without cause. Of course, we can pick up vibes from others, but it's better not to make assumptions. Insecurity has a voice, as does trauma. It tells you what other people are thinking, but not everything we believe is correct.

I understand that I am not everybody's flavour and vice versa. Unless someone says they do not like me, I infer indifference. If it bothers me that much, I ask questions to get to know the other person better. I will not force anyone to like me, but I will be civil. I am not naturally extroverted, which may give off the wrong impression so, I give people the benefit of the doubt, as that's how I would like to be treated.

Do not chase after people. I know it can be hard, but I believe that friends should meet us halfway. It hurts when you're constantly trying to connect with someone who isn't giving you the time of day. We must know when to draw the line.

Take a step back and think:

Is this relationship honouring or helping me grow in any way?

You may need to assess the relationship, not everyone who calls you their friend is your friend, but everyone serves a purpose. Perhaps they are just someone who you are supposed to be a blessing to for a season. Although, I use the word 'friend' loosely, I know where to place people in my life. Whether they are acquaintances, close friends or confidants, they all serve a purpose in my life of which I value. It's up to me to assess the role they play and 'move with wisdom' as my friend Nellia would say.

Chapter 12: While you are waiting

Almost Love

To be loved is to be fully known and still be accepted.

I feel for us women. I do because we are extraordinary beings. We feel so much and give so much of ourselves.

I'm the type of woman to love with everything. If I decide to commit, it will be to one man for the rest of my life; and I will love him till we go home. It's in my wiring.

But why do I seem to attract manipulators – men who seek to control me – when all I want is to be loved?

The truth is, I want someone to see into the depths of my soul and choose me. I want someone to decide and choose to love me because I've always felt like other people are obliged to love me. Sometimes, I even feel God has no choice but to love me because that is His nature. I desire one person to fight for me and never give up on me.

We love the idea of love that never fails. We say clichés like "If it's meant to be. It will be" because we secretly still believe in a happily-ever-after. I know I do. Even when I push someone away, I want them to tell me what we have is special and worth fighting for. And I'm disappointed when they don't.

I loved the attention David gave me because he did something no one had ever done before. He told me bedtime stories, something I never experienced with my Father as a child. It was comforting. I wasn't initially seeking his attention, but I started to crave it once it was gone.

Even after we stopped talking, he consumed my thoughts. I just wanted love so badly. Love that was already freely given to me by God on the cross.

Be intentional about your healing

I'm realising just how important it is for us women to be intentional about healing from any undealt childhood trauma we have. As well as praying, I also recommend journaling and even speaking to a therapist. Had David not entered my life, I wouldn't have known I had these issues I needed to heal from.

Maybe you're not in love. Perhaps you attached yourself out of need and desperation. Or you might just fear being alone.

It may be illogical that I was willing to give up everything for David, but I sometimes get tired of things making sense. I want a love that doesn't make sense. I believe the power of two people in love, not lust, can overcome any barrier or obstacle.

I think about how good my parents looked together, how things started well for them, and everybody telling me they loved each other. Why didn't it work? I believe it was because God was not the foundation. If God, who is love, is the foundation, any relationship can last if the two people are willing to continuously put Him first. I don't want to risk things not working out because I refused to listen to wisdom's instruction. I wanted David to understand. When you've been through what I have, you don't want to take any chances.

Deep down, I know that I wasn't the problem. We were people with different values, and he just wasn't the man I needed.

The type of marriage I dream of can only be accomplished with God at the centre. Even with the best intentions, without the right foundation, some things are destined to fail. I want my marriage to last a lifetime. I don't ever want to separate from or divorce my spouse.

I want a man who knows how to protect my purity and believes in waiting to have sex till we are married. I know this man is rare, but I'm hoping he does exist. I still remember the way David looked at me that day at the train station. His eyes said it all. I wonder if Jesus ever looks at me like that; with such passion and intensity. Like I'm the only woman in the world.

They say a man knows when he has found 'the one', but they never say what happens to a woman. Although men are the pursuers, we must remember that us women also have options. We don't have to settle for any scraps we are given.

Having high standards

The Bible teaches that husbands should love their wives like Christ loved the church – **He gave up his life for her** (Ephesians 5:25). This is our standard for love as women of God, but how easily do we give our hearts to men who don't deserve it?

Stop playing hard to get and become hard to get!

Men like a mystery, so remember not to reveal too much about yourself during the early stages of talking. Because if some men think they can suss you out, they'll become too familiar and try to take advantage of you. I'm speaking from experience! I don't believe you can teach somebody else's son what it means to be a gentleman, but you can give him some tips.

When I was twenty-two, I was talking to a young man who had implied he had wanted to develop a closer friendship with me. I told him I don't talk on the phone past midnight. I knew from experience just how crazy late-night conversations could get, so I had to set the tone of the friendship, and I could tell he respected me for it. We reached a stage where we would talk, and he

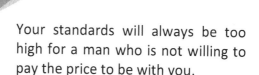

Your standards will always be too high for a man who is not willing to pay the price to be with you.

would say 'it's coming up to 12 now, so I'm going to let you go.'

It was my way of not blurring the boundaries of our friendship, and, I found it easier to control any feelings I was developing for him.

Boundaries prevent you from making silly mistakes

When we are young, we think our parents set boundaries because they are mean and want to control our lives. However, as we mature, we understand that they were just trying to protect us. It's the same with God. His commandments are there to safeguard our lives. The Bible repeatedly reminds us that our actions have consequences, just like any good parent would.

Remember well, the next time you willingly choose to disobey God. It's his world; since he designed it, he knows what works best! It takes humility to think this way. I haven't always gotten this right, but I'm learning from past failures. Remember, 'God opposes the proud but gives grace to the humble' (James 4:6 NLT).

Remember how I said you teach people how to treat you? What you allow in the early stages of any relationship will set the tone for the course of the relationship, so be mindful of red flags. If the person does not respect the small boundaries you set at these early stages, they may have ulterior motives.

Remember: 'Wisdom is the principal thing, therefore get wisdom: with all thy getting get understanding '(Proverbs 4:7).

God takes no delight in our mishaps, but He delights in our prosperity. Knowledge is free, but knowledge is only powerful when you use it.

When considering a life partner

Your standards will always be too high for a man who is not willing to pay the price to be with you.

I'm not talking about material things here. I believe some women substitute a man's values for his status and material possessions. While it is true that love gives, it appears some men today hold more affection for money than for us women, so we believe that if you spend your money on us, we have a piece of your heart. However, this can go wrong because certain men, especially those with lots of money to spare, will just use this to get what they want.

The price I'm talking about is patience and purity; therefore, an important characteristic to look for in a partner is self-control.

Sometimes we're scared to tell people what we truly want because we're not sure if they'll be willing to give it to us. Part of knowing your worth is to be unapologetic and uncompromising about your beliefs. Is it me, or do some men think we are asking too much when we want to wait till after marriage to have sex?

It may be old-fashioned, traditional and, even amongst believers, far from the norm in today's society, but, growing up, I was always taught that a woman was 'worth the wait'. It was romanticised and more respected. The older I get, the more I realise how much the world has changed and is continually evolving. I believe we are living in the last days. I understand that people are getting married later in life, which is valid since marriage isn't something to be rushed into.

Being a '30-year-old' unmarried virgin today has negative connotations. It can make you feel something is wrong with you or that you're undesirable. But, sis, you're a diamond; don't let anyone treat you like a plastic bag. You are not disposable goods or a garbage dump for someone's emotional baggage, especially if you've already taken the time to work on yourself.

Remember, hurting people hurt people, so be discerning when choosing who to entertain. You should ask God what your assignment is, as this will help you discern whether a man you are interested in is right for you.

This is bigger than you.

Write down what you want in a partner

If a man is not committed and submitted to God, I cannot expect him to commit to me, and I cannot trust him enough to submit to him. Where purpose is unknown, abuse is inevitable.

The man I desire must exhibit the qualities I admire:

Gentleness

Faithfulness

Love

Joy

Peace

Patience

Self-
Control

Humility

Integrity

Where purpose is unknown, abuse is inevitable.

-Myles Monroe, Understanding the Purpose and Power of Woman

However, this is not to say that I am looking for a perfect partner, because I am not perfect, no one is. I am just looking for someone who has a sincere desire to grow in the fruits of the spirit.

Be the real deal

I am a rare woman, not just because people have said this to me, but because I recognise my distinction amongst women, in the way I think which is demonstrated in the way I conduct myself. Believe me when I say I am the real deal. I have worked on myself and sacrificed to be closer to God. I may not always get it right, but I have tried to walk closely with him, and that alone sets me apart.

Because I've adopted traits like gentleness and compassion, I attract all sorts of men. I understand that people are looking for God, but only He can save their souls; I don't have the power to change anyone. Trying to change someone will just leave you feeling burnt out and drained. My mistakes have taught me that it isn't wise to date someone less spiritually mature than me. I believe God calls men to be leaders of their homes, so, my husband must be able to lead me spiritually. If I don't feel safe, if I don't see how a man can lead me spiritually, then I can't form a relationship with that man because I do not know who or what governs him.

As a woman who will submit to her husband (some say before marriage), I need to know to whom he is submitted to feel comfortable enough to trust him. Although marriage is an equal partnership and we have different roles, the man is the head. Everything we do comes from our heads: where we go, what we wear and say.

Is he worthy of your trust? What governs the decisions he makes? Who influences his thinking? Is he motivated by lust, ego and pride; or by love, servitude and humility? These are questions that need answering about the man we allow to lead us. Without asking directly, we can usually discover the answers through observation and evaluation.

A man whose thoughts and attitudes are not governed by God and who is not consistently working on renewing his mind by the word of God is dangerous to a godly, high-value woman. Whether we like it or not, men being the logical thinkers they are, usually lead a relationship. Abuse is real, and a man who does not yield his emotions to God may lack self-control. A lack of self-control can lead to violent outbursts. They may start small, but those angry outbursts must be controlled before they become fits of rage. This is true for both men and women.

Possessing wisdom gives you foresight. Whenever I'm watching a movie, I can sometimes predict the ending or a plot twist because I'm a storyteller, and I also studied media at A-Level. The same is true when you possess godly wisdom, it warns you of the dangers ahead. If you don't have it, ask God, and he'll give it to you. In my life – I can usually tell how a relationship will end depending on the red flags that come up during our interactions. Some would say I'm prophetic, but I think I'm just highly intuitive based on life experience. I notice patterns and patterns don't lie.

Which leads me to my next point: A man who hasn't completely healed from his previous relationship cannot love you properly. Not in the way you need and deserve to be loved.

The case of the ex

History often repeats itself unless an individual is willing to do the inner work to change the outcome.

Beware of familiarity. The chances are, this guy won't be able to value and respect you because, at the back of his mind, he's comparing your good and bad points with hers. He won't take the time to figure you out because, in his head, 'all women are the same'.

So, he will tell you what you want to hear. At first, he'll flatter you. He might even say you being nothing like his ex is what drew him to you in the first place until you do something that feels familiar to him. Deep down, he believed you were just like his ex. He was just hoping you would be a better version.

You may even subconsciously start acting out of character in trying to prove him wrong, but it becomes a self-fulfilling prophecy. You will end up feeling 'not good enough' for him because *she* wasn't. Now you're paying for somebody else's mistakes.

You deserve better. Let go and move on.

You will shine

There are a thousand other girls in the room, but you will shine.

You will shine

You will shine like a shining star.

Yes, you will shine

You might think they're so much better than you,

Prettier, smarter, cooler than you

But trust me, my child, you will shine

He won't be looking at your hair, your clothes or your exterior

But he will be looking at your heart

Wait for love

Because you will shine brighter than any flame, any star, any light

You will shine

He will be looking at the beauty that comes from your laugh, your smile and your spirit.

The unfading beauty, the treasure buried deep within you, and your beauty will radiate like the morning sun

And he will choose you because he can clearly see the God in you.

Wait my love

Wait my child

You will shine, and you will be beautiful, more beautiful than any earthly thing,

More beautiful than you could even imagine, the beauty of God is within you.

Words cannot describe HIS beauty, majesty and glory, that same presence you possess. Trust in the presence of God that lives in you.

He will come, and you will shine.

(October 2012)

Times and seasons - a time for everything

If the motive behind wanting to get married is to make your friends jealous, you have a problem.

If you plan to get married because you feel incomplete, you have a problem.

The purpose of marriage is to glorify God.

The truth is we were not all born on the same day, year, minute and hour. Just like we didn't all graduate at the same time. Some people did not even decide to go to university to study; this is because everybody's journey is different.

I felt as if I was behind in life because I had to take a year out from university due to my mental breakdown, but when I graduated, none of that mattered. I was just happy that it was finally my time.

Living a life of Purity

'How can a young man keep his way pure? By guarding it according to your word' (Psalm 119:9)

Purity requires intentionality, self-discipline and accountability. God is not pleased that you've managed to remain a virgin or celibate; God is pleased when you have stayed pure. Nothing has to occur physically for it to happen in your mind and heart.

According to Lexico.com, to be pure means to be without mixture 'not mixed or adulterated with any other substance or material.' [7]

The only way for young people to do this is through prayer and to daily, continually, practice the art of renewing your mind with the word of God and doing what it says (Please read **James 1:22-25**), because temptations are everywhere. One only has to look on social media to be tempted to envy or lust.

---

[7] https://www.lexico.com/definition/pure

If we do not meditate daily on His word and allow it to take root in and influence our hearts, minds, and actions, we will be led astray by the god of this world. I am speaking from experience.

Chapter 13: She laughs without fear of the future

Letter to Myself

Dearest Ebony,

Lies look like the truth when you don't know what the truth looks like.

Lust looks like love when you don't know what love is.

As a dog returns to its vomit, fools repeat their folly[8].

Take a minute, let that sink in.

Don't allow your feelings to lead you where God has not sent you.

Baby girl, I know you sometimes get impatient, but God knows your situation.

Young lady, I know you feel stuck right now

You're finding it difficult to let go emotionally

But believe me, when I tell you, you have moved on

Don't feel bad about the length of time it took you to move on

---

[8] Proverbs 26:11

It was necessary

You chose to give someone you hoped would be in your life for a long time a chance

You built a bond and became emotionally invested

But believe me when I tell you, you have moved on

There was a reason you decided to let this person go

Don't look back. Don't seek closure

Stop stalking his social media page

You will not find thoughts of you there

You are not the Almighty

Only God truly knows another human being's thoughts

You must be determined to keep moving on

Minding your own business…

Baby girl, I know the future looks uncertain right now, but when has anything ever been certain?

I mean, how did you even get here?

Did you predict that you would be in the middle of a global pandemic in 2020?

The answer is no.

You must look forward.

You must see with the eyes of faith now more than ever.

Believe and hold onto hope for your future.

Don't rush to find someone else to fill the gap that he left. You will be hugely disappointed.

Take your time. You're building something here.

Just like Noah, you're building something that will keep you and your loved ones safe when the next trial hits the earth.

(May 2020)

Deciding to be great can be difficult

As a Christian, you're not going to be perfect, but growing in Christ requires moral excellence. You must rise above mediocrity which gets HARD at times.

I keep hearing the phrase, 'what's ahead is greater than what's behind us' during this season. Despite the difficulties, we press on because we know a greater inheritance lies ahead. We often dwell in the past because what lies ahead seems so uncertain, but that's why we must remind ourselves of God's promises.

Moving forward, however, requires us to be responsible and accountable for our everyday decisions. There is no glory without responsibility. There's no escaping the process, but we need to endure because the result will be beautiful; just like when a caterpillar becomes a butterfly. 'But the one who endures to the end shall be saved' (Matthew 24:13).

While setting goals is important, we need to remember who is in charge.

> 'Now listen, you who say, "Today or tomorrow we will go to this or that city, spend a year there, carry on business and make money." Why, you do not even know what will happen tomorrow. What is your life? You are a mist that appears for a little while and then vanishes. Instead, you ought to say, 'If it is the Lord's will, we will live and do this or that' (James 4:13-15).

If the year 2020 has taught me anything, it's this Scripture right here – 'Many are the plans in a person's heart, but it's the LORD's purpose that prevails' (Proverbs 19:21).

For the first time in recent history, we faced a global pandemic where everything stopped. To stop the spread of the virus, schools and shops closed and people were quarantined, confined to only leaving their houses to exercise and go grocery shopping. I am finishing this book during this pandemic.

The virus has affected everything: over a million people have died worldwide. People lost their jobs; many self-employed people have seen their income come to a halt. Entrepreneurs have also had to re-strategize; weddings have been postponed, and many remain fearful.

We need to hold on to our faith in God's word now more than ever. Everything that could be shaken has, this has resulted in not only the church, but the entire world, having to 'Be still and know that He is God'.

The Bible gives God's children the following reasons not to fear: 'Even though I walk through the darkest valley, I will fear no evil, for you are with me; your rod and your staff, they comfort me' (Psalms 23:4).

> 1. 'Whoever dwells in the shelter of the Most High will rest in the shadow of the Almighty. I will say of the LORD, "He is my refuge and my fortress, my God, in whom I trust." Surely, he will save you from the fowler's snare and from the deadly pestilence. He will cover you with his feathers, and under his wings, you will find refuge; his faithfulness will be your shield and rampart. You will not fear the terror of night, nor the arrow that flies by day, nor the pestilence that stalks in the darkness, nor the plague that destroys at midday. A thousand may fall at your side, ten thousand at your right hand, but it will not come near you. You will only observe with your eyes and see the punishment of the wicked.

> 'If you say, "The LORD is my refuge," and you make the Most High your dwelling, no

harm will overtake you, no disaster will come near your tent. For he will command his angels concerning you to guard you in all your ways; they will lift you up in their hands so that you will not strike your foot against a stone. You will tread on the lion and the cobra; you will trample the great lion and the serpent.

"Because he loves me," says the LORD, "I will rescue him; I will protect him, for he acknowledges my name. He will call on me, and I will answer him; I will be with him in trouble, I will deliver him and honour him. With long life, I will satisfy him and show him my salvation"' (Psalm 91 NIV).

2. '"For I know the plans I have for you," declares the Lord, "plans to prosper you and not to harm you, plans to give you hope and a future"' (Jeremiah 29:11).

We have had to *set our minds on the things above – and guard our thought life – whatsoever is lovely, [etc.] ... think about such things*[9].

As humans, we are naturally inclined to think negatively. We must train our minds to meditate on the right things. Many books teach this. There are ideologies out there like: *The Law of Attraction, Think and Grow Rich,* and *Raising your Vibration,* all with

---

[9] Philippians 4:8

biblical principles. 'However, NOTHING, absolutely nothing compares to the living word of God.

All Scripture is inspired by God.[10]

As we discipline ourselves to meditate on the word of God, the Holy Spirit will play his part and bring these things to our remembrance at the right time.

Remember everything will be okay, in the end. If it's not okay, it's not the end.

His Masterpiece: She is worth more than diamonds

'You're a dime plus 99, and it's a shame you don't even know what you're worth.'

Oh, but she's willing to learn... Still the same woman but different.

Life is teaching me old lessons in new ways.

She's broken... but stable.

Compassionate but fierce.

Loyal but discerning.

She stands for and wears the truth securely around her waist.

Uncertain but pushing forward regardless.

Her prayers are sometimes tears... but carry power and weight.

---

[10] 2 Timothy 3:16

Her only desire is to do what is right.

She's willing to break barriers and glass ceilings because she knows a generation depends on her obedience.

Her faith surrounds her as a shield of protection

She lifts up her head.

She wears the Helmet of Salvation.

Her only weapon is the word of God as a Sword.

Wherever she treads, she brings good news.

She is worth more than diamonds.

She is me.

Conclusion

Knowing our worth and not settling for anything less than God's best is a process that takes submission and surrendering to God's plan. Like you, I am still on a journey of understanding my worth in God.

During the course of writing this book, I was tested in this area. I had to ask myself a pivotal question: 'What precedent will I be setting for my children and grandchildren if I give up now?' I often hear Christians talk about breaking generational curses... but guess what? Poverty is a curse; sexual sin is a curse; divorce is a curse. Abuse is a curse. When the enemy comes to tempt me with any of these and more, I must remember what and who I am fighting for. I am fighting, not just for me, but for the next generation, and I am determined to **WIN.**

I can finally say I am in love with the woman I am becoming.

With Love,

Ebony Ali

If you would like more information about myself or would like to enquire about the services I provide, please visit: www.ebonyali.com.

Bibliography

Chapter Six
1. Oxford Dictionary

Chapter Seven
1. Jonathan McReynolds - Lovin' Me (Official Video, 2013). Available at https://www.youtube.com/watch?v=mfyVeJ2OdQg Accessed 30/07/2020

Chapter Eight
1. Where Is the Love? Lyrics by Black Eyed Peas - Lyrics On Demand Available at http://www.lyricsondemand.com/b//blackeyedpeas lyrics/whereisthelovelyrics.html Accessed 09/09/2020

Chapter Ten
1. Address by Nelson Mandela for the "Make Poverty History" Campaign, London - United Kingdom (3 February 2005) Available at http://www.mandela.gov.za/mandela_speeches/200 5/050203_poverty.htm Accessed 09/09/2020
2. Tony Evans - https://tonyevans.org/when-god-lets-you-hit-rock-bottom/ Accessed 11/09/2020

Chapter Eleven
1. E.E. Cummings - https://www.goodreads.com/quotes/806-it-takes-courage-to-grow-up-and-become-who-you Accessed 11/09/2020
2. Rachel Kerr – https://www.youtube.com/watch?v=F4_0efzhzJ4 Accessed 26/09/2020

Chapter Twelve

1. https://www.lexico.com/definition/pure Accessed 15/09/2020

Other Helpful Links:

https://financesonline.com/10--expensive-gemstones-from-tanzanite-to-pink-star-diamond/

https://www.forbes.com/sites/trevornace/2015/11/02/12-most-expensive-gemstones-world/#574712031538

https://www.withclarity.com/blog/2019/10/16/what-are-diamonds-made-of/

https://myhealth.alberta.ca/health/Pages/conditions.aspx?hwid=tp10241

https://www.goodreads.com/quotes/688275-when-purpose-is-not-known-abuse-is-inevitable#:~:text=Quote%20by%20Myles%20Munroe%3A%20%E2%80%9CWhen,not%20known%2C%20abuse%20is%20inevitable%E2%80%9D

Printed in Great Britain
by Amazon

54649657R00127